Municipal Public Employment
and Public Expenditure

Municipal Public Employment and Public Expenditure

Richard D. Gustely
Virginia Polytechnic Institute
and State University

Lexington Books
D.C. Heath and Company
Lexington, Massachusetts
Toronto   London

Library of Congress Cataloging in Publication Data

Gustely, Richard D.
    Municipal public employment and public expenditure.

    Bibliography: p.
    1. Municipal   officials   and   employees—United   States—Salaries,
allowances, etc. 2. Municipal finance—United States. I. Title.
JS361.G88   352'.005'120973   74-22044
ISBN 0-669-96867-6

Published simultaneously in Canada.

Printed in the United States of America.

International Standard Book Number: 0-669-96867-6

Library of Congress Catalog Card Number: 74-22044

For Mary Lou

Contents

List of Tables

Preface

Among the most important causes of the present municipal fiscal crisis are the suburbanization of the white middle-class and the concentration of the poor and the black in our central cities. The effect of this migration has been to lower the municipal tax base and to increase demands on the local public sector to provide additional services. However, the lack of a generally accepted positive theory of local expenditure has made the prescription of "remedies" for this crisis difficult because of the inability to predict the effect of the "remedies" on local government behavior.

Because of the lack of such a positive theory, and spurred on by the intensity of the crisis, analyses have been undertaken to identify the determinants of local (and state) fiscal activity. This literature has focused in three areas—public expenditures, public employment, and public wages. However, because of their limited scope these studies have produced little understanding of the expenditure determination process, of which employment and wage determination are an integral part.

The purpose here, then, is to integrate these parts into a model of the municipal expenditure determination process and to test its validity empirically. It is felt that this analysis will lead to a greater understanding of local public-sector fiscal activity, and will enable policymakers to predict the effects of their prescriptions more easily.

This research grew out of my work at the Metropolitan Research Center at Syracuse University while I was on the staff of the Maxwell Research Project on the Public Finances of New York City. I am grateful to Roy Bahl for the many hours he spent with me in the discussion of the material contained in this study, to Jesse Burkhead, David Greytak, and Seymour Sacks for their helpful comments on the original draft; and to the Bureau of the Census-Governments Division for providing me with fiscal data in advance of their publication. Finally, special thanks are due to my wife, Mary Lou, for her patience in those trying times of manuscript preparation and revision.

1

The Setting for Analyzing Municipal Fiscal Behavior

Dimensions of the Municipal Fiscal Crisis

Citizen demands on the municipal public sector, while always great, have accelerated in the past decade. The poor have been calling for more public services to be provided; the rich have been demanding relief from the heavy burden of the property tax; and all have been criticizing municipal government for being both unresponsive and inefficient. Faced with these difficulties, local officials have turned to the federal government for assistance, only to be told that war and inflation have drained federal fiscal resources to the point that little money is left for relief of the municipal fiscal crisis.

The complexity of the fiscal dilemma faced by local public officials can be seen by analyzing the composition of municipal public expenditures over time. (See Tables 1-1, 1-2, and 1-3). Because of the service nature of most of the output of the local public sector, production is relatively labor intensive with payroll costs representing substantial fractions of total expenditure (Table 1-1). Further, while a wide range of services are provided by most municipalities, a large portion of employment is concentrated in those functions (police, fire, education, and so forth) which are generally believed to be characterized by price inelastic demand and which pay above average wage rates (Table 1-2). Finally, rather than stabilizing, growth in the local public sector seems to be increasing, as evidenced by the accelerating growth rates of wages, employment, payrolls, and expenditures between 1957 and 1972 (Table 1-3).

In light of these facts, it appears that any hope of alleviating the local fiscal crisis requires first an understanding of the factors that influence municipal spending, that is, an understanding of the expenditure determination process. Further, the diverse nature of the components of public expenditure suggest the necessity of understanding the relationship of wage, employment, and nonpayroll cost determination in this process.

Limitations of Previous Studies

Beginning with the work of Solomon Fabricant (21) and Harvey Brazer (17), numerous studies have been undertaken over the past thirty years to identify the determinants of local government expenditure patterns using both cross-

1

Table 1-1

The Functional Distribution of Total Expenditure and Payroll Cost Levels of all Municipal Governments in the United States: 1957, 1962, 1967, 1972 (in Millions of Dollars and Percentages)

Functions	1957 Payroll	% of Total	Expend-iture	% of Total	1962 Payroll	% of Total	Expend-iture	% of Total	1967 Payroll	% Dist.	Expend-iture	% of Total	1972 Payroll	% of Total	Expend-iture	% of Total
Education	1,021	18.46	1,423	11.70	1,540	19.38	1,925	11.63	2,431	20.87	3,140	12.92	4,225	21.30	5,767	13.80
Highways	368	6.65	1,313	10.79	526	6.62	1,690	10.21	659	5.66	2,001	8.23	988	4.98	2,787	6.67
Public Welfare	70	1.27	489	4.02	109	1.37	686	4.15	234	2.01	1,226	5.04	361	1.82	2,992	7.16
Hospitals	303	5.48	529	4.35	425	5.35	692	4.18	603	5.18	1,028	4.23	1,017	5.13	2,049	4.90
Health	98	1.77	159	1.31	134	1.69	182	1.10	176	1.51	255	1.05	324	1.63	669	1.60
Police	880	15.91	1,041	8.56	1,268	15.95	1,472	8.90	1,884	16.17	2,039	8.39	3,575	18.02	3,958	9.47
Fire	571	10.32	709	5.83	817	10.28	986	5.96	1,190	10.21	1,300	5.35	2,001	10.09	2,216	5.30
Sewer & Sewerage Disposal	132	2.39	642	5.28	167	2.10	850	5.14	230	1.97	1,084	4.46	390	1.97	1,916	4.59
Other Sanitation	287	5.19	504	4.14	440	5.54	624	3.77	591	5.07	790	3.25	880	4.44	1,341	3.21
Parks & Recreation	194	3.51	459	3.77	306	3.85	635	3.84	423	3.63	905	3.72	708	3.57	1,561	3.74
Housing & Urban Renewal	39	0.70	247	2.03	75	0.94	635	3.84	145	1.24	808	3.32	308	1.55	1,482	3.55
Air Transportation	14	0.25	105	0.86	24	0.30	192	1.16	39	0.33	201	0.83	73	0.37	532	1.27
Water Transportation	23	0.42	47	0.39	18	0.23	77	0.47	18	0.15	61	0.25	33	0.17	163	0.39
Correction	24	0.43	NA	NA	56	0.70	96	0.58	83	0.71	119	0.49	143	0.72	232	0.56
Libraries	80	1.45	145	1.19	119	1.50	210	1.27	180	1.55	302	1.24	277	1.40	464	1.11
General Control	436	7.88	512	4.21	297	3.74	401	2.42	476	4.09	549	2.26	870	4.39	993	2.38

Financial Administration	NAa	NAa	NAa	NAa	225	2.83	247	1.49	292	2.51	331	1.36	478	2.41	570	1.36
Water Supply	311	5.62	1,305	10.73	406	5.11	1,567	9.47	515	4.42	1,898	7.81	723	3.65	2,622	6.28
Electric Power	182	3.29	844	6.94	248	3.12	1,016	6.14	317	2.72	1,847	7.60	456	2.30	2,312	5.53
Transit	255	4.61	487	4.00	296	3.72	533	3.22	501	4.30	1,285	5.29	674	3.40	1,176	2.81
Gas	14	0.25	110	0.90	39	0.49	149	0.90	31	0.27	287	1.18	49	0.25	273	0.65
General Public Buildings	NA	NA	157	1.29	NA	NA	206	1.24	NA	NA	330	1.36	NA	NA	527	1.26
Interest on General Debt	NA	NA	309	2.54	NA	NA	512	3.09	NA	NA	745	3.06	NA	NA	1,537	3.68
Other & Unallocable	230	4.16	628	5.16	413	5.20	965	5.83	632	5.42	1,781	7.33	1,281	6.46	3,642	8.72
Total	5,532	100.01	12,164	99.99	7,948	100.01	16,548	100.00	11,650	99.99	24,312	100.02	19,834	100.32	41,781	99.9

aIncluded in general control.

Source: *Census of Governments*, 1957, 1962, 1967 and 1972, U.S. Department of Commerce.

Table 1-2

The Functional Distribution of Employment Levels and Wage Rates of all Municipal Governments in the United States: 1957, 1962, 1967, 1972 (Employment in Thousands, Wages in Dollars)

Functions	1957				1962				1967				1972			
	Employment	% of Total	Wages	% of Average	Employment	% of Total	Wages	% of Average	Employment	% of Total	Wages	% of Average	Employment	% of Total	Wages	% of Average
Education	192	14.79	5,318	124.78	227	15.31	6,784	126.59	306	17.87	7,944	116.74	378	18.64	11,177	114.28
Highways	102	7.86	3,608	84.66	108	7.28	4,870	90.88	111	6.48	5,937	87.24	119	5.87	8,303	84.90
Public Welfare	18	1.39	3,890	91.27	22	1.48	4,955	92.46	37	2.16	6,324	92.93	43	2.12	8,395	85.84
Hospitals	104	8.01	2,913	68.35	111	7.48	3,829	71.45	118	6.89	5,110	75.09	129	6.36	7,884	80.61
Health	24	1.85	4,083	95.80	25	1.69	5,360	100.02	27	1.58	6,519	95.80	37	1.82	8,757	89.54
Police	198	15.25	4,444	104.27	224	15.10	5,661	105.64	258	15.07	7,302	107.30	319	15.73	11,207	114.59
Fire	122	9.40	4,680	109.81	140	9.44	5,836	108.90	157	9.17	7,580	111.39	181	8.93	11,055	113.04
Sewers & Sewerage Disposal	36	2.77	3,667	86.04	35	2.36	4,771	89.03	40	2.34	5,750	84.50	46	2.27	8,478	86.69
Other Sanitation	78	6.01	3,679	86.32	99	6.68	4,444	82.93	108	6.31	5,472	80.41	109	5.37	8,073	82.55
Parks & Recreation	54	4.16	3,593	84.30	69	4.65	4,435	82.76	78	4.56	5,423	79.69	89	4.39	7,955	81.34
Housing & Urban Renewal	9	0.69	4,333	101.67	14	0.94	5,357	99.96	19	1.11	7,632	112.15	31	1.53	9,935	101.58
Air Transportation	4	0.31	3,500	82.12	5	0.34	4,800	89.57	6	0.35	6,500	95.52	8	0.39	9,125	93.30
Water Transportation	5	0.39	4,600	107.93	3	0.20	6,000	111.96	2	0.12	9,000	132.26	3	0.15	11,000	112.47
Corrections	5	0.39	4,800	112.62	10	0.67	5,600	104.50	11	0.64	7,545	110.87	15	0.74	9,533	97.47
Libraries	21	1.62	3,810	89.39	28	1.89	4,250	79.31	34	1.99	5,294	77.80	36	1.78	7,694	78.67
General Control	94	7.24	4,638	108.82	54	3.64	5,500	102.63	71	4.15	6,704	98.52	91	4.49	9,560	97.75
Financial Administration	NAa	NAa	NAa	NAa	47	3.17	4,787	89.33	47	2.75	6,213	91.30	55	2.71	8,691	88.87
Water Supply	80	6.16	3,888	91.22	83	5.60	4,892	91.29	84	4.91	6,131	90.10	84	4.14	8,607	88.01

5

Electric Power	41	3.16	4,439	104.15	42	2.83	5,905	110.19	43	2.51	7,372	108.33	44	2.17	10,364	105.97
Transit	52	4.01	4,904	115.06	47	3.17	6,298	117.52	52	3.04	9,635	141.59	55	2.71	12,255	125.31
Gas	4	0.31	3,500	82.12	8	0.54	4,875	90.97	5	0.29	6,200	91.11	6	0.30	8,167	83.51
General Public Buildings	NA	NA	NA	NA	NA	NA	NA	NA	NA	NA	NA	NA	NA	NA	NA	NA
Interest on General Debt	NA	NA	NA	NA	NA	NA	NA	NA	NA	NA	NA	NA	NA	NA	NA	NA
Other & Unallocable	55	4.24	4,182	98.12	82	5.53	5,037	93.99	98	5.72	6,449	94.77	150	7.40	8,540	87.32
Total (ave.)	1,298	100.01	(4,262)	(100.00)	1,483	99.99	(5,359)	(100.00)	1,712	100.01	(6,805)	(100.00)	2,028	100.01	(9,780)	(100.00)

aIncluded in general control.
Source: *Census of Governments*, 1957, 1962, 1967 and 1972, U.S. Department of Commerce.

Table 1-3
The Functional Distribution of Growth in Expenditure, Payroll, Employment, and Wages of all Municipal Government in the United States: 1957-1972 (as Percentages)

Functions	1957-1962 Expenditure	Payroll	Employment	Wages	1962-1967 Expenditure	Payroll	Employment	Wages	1967-1972 Expenditure	Payroll	Employment	Wages	1957-1972 Expenditure	Payroll	Employment	Wages
Education	35.28	50.83	18.23	27.57	29.17	57.86	34.80	17.10	83.66	73.80	23.53	40.70	305.27	313.81	96.88	110.17
Highways	28.71	42.93	5.88	34.98	18.40	25.29	2.78	21.91	39.28	49.92	7.21	39.85	112.26	168.48	16.67	130.13
Public Welfare	40.29	55.71	22.22	27.38	78.72	114.68	68.18	27.63	144.05	54.27	16.22	32.75	511.86	415.71	138.89	115.81
Hospitals	30.81	40.26	6.73	31.45	48.55	41.88	6.31	33.46	99.32	68.66	9.32	54.29	287.33	235.64	24.04	170.65
Health	14.47	36.73	4.17	31.28	40.11	31.34	8.00	21.62	132.65	84.09	37.04	34.33	320.75	230.61	54.17	114.47
Police	41.40	44.09	13.13	27.39	38.52	48.58	15.18	28.99	94.11	89.76	23.64	53.48	280.21	349.77	61.11	152.18
Fire	39.07	43.08	14.75	24.70	31.85	45.65	12.14	29.88	70.46	68.15	15.29	45.84	212.55	288.09	48.36	136.22
Sewers & Sewerage Disposal	32.40	26.52	-2.78	30.11	27.53	37.72	14.29	20.52	76.75	69.57	15.00	47.44	198.44	195.45	27.78	131.20
Other Sanitation	23.81	53.31	26.92	20.79	26.60	34.32	9.09	23.13	69.76	48.90	9.25	47.53	166.07	206.62	39.74	119.43
Parks & Recreation	38.34	57.73	27.78	23.43	42.52	38.24	13.04	22.28	72.49	67.38	14.10	46.69	240.01	264.95	64.81	121.40
Housing & Urban Renewal	157.09	92.31	55.56	23.63	27.24	93.33	35.71	42.47	83.42	112.41	63.16	30.18	500.00	689.74	244.44	129.29
Air Transportation	82.86	71.43	25.00	37.14	4.69	62.50	20.00	35.42	164.68	87.18	33.33	40.38	406.67	421.83	100.00	160.71
Water Transportation	63.83	-21.74	-40.00	30.43	-20.78	0.00	-33.34	50.00	167.21	83.33	50.00	22.22	246.81	43.48	-40.00	139.13
Corrections	—	133.33	100.00	16.67	23.96	48.21	10.00	34.73	94.96	72.29	36.36	26.35	141.67[b]	495.83	200.00	98.60
Libraries	44.83	48.75	33.33	11.55	43.81	51.26	21.43	24.56	53.64	53.89	5.88	45.33	220.00	246.25	71.43	101.94
General Control	26.56	19.72	7.45	11.43	36.91	60.27	31.48	21.89	80.87	82.77	28.17	42.60	205.27	209.17	55.32	99.07
Financial Administration	a	a	a	a	34.01	29.78	0.00	29.79	72.21	63.70	17.02	39.88	a	a	a	a
Water Supply	20.08	30.55	3.75	25.82	21.12	26.85	1.20	25.33	38.15	40.39	0.00	40.38	100.92	132.48	5.00	121.37

Electric Power	20.38	36.26	2.44	33.03	81.79	27.82	2.38	24.84	25.18	43.85	2.33	40.59	173.93	150.55	7.32 133.48
Transit	9.45	16.08	-9.62	28.43	141.09	69.26	10.64	52.99	-8.49	34.53	5.77	27.19	141.48	164.31	5.77 149.90
Gas	35.45	178.57	100.00	39.29	92.62	-20.51	-37.50	27.18	-4.88	58.06	20.00	31.73	148.18	250.00	50.00 133.34
General Public Buildings	31.21	NA	NA	NA	60.19	NA	NA	NA	59.70	NA	NA	NA	235.67	NA	NA NA
Interest on General Debt	65.70	NA	NA	NA	45.51	NA	NA	NA	106.31	NA	NA	NA	397.41	NA	NA NA
Other & Unallocable	53.66	79.57	49.09	20.44	84.56	53.03	19.51	28.03	104.49	102.69	53.06	32.42	479.94	456.96	172.73 104.21
Total	36.04	43.67	14.25	25.74	46.92	46.58	15.44	26.98	71.85	70.25	18.46	43.72	243.48	258.53	56.24 129.47

aIncluded in general control.
bCalculated for 1962-1972.
Source: *Census of Governments*, 1957, 1962, 1967 and 1972, U.S. Department of Commerce.

sectional and time-series data.[a] The approach employed in most of these studies has been to regress per capita expenditures for some level of government upon such variables as per capita income, population density, and per capita intergovernmental aid, and to identify variables with statistically significant coefficients as determinants.

This approach has been criticized because of three conceptual and statistical limitations.[b] First, the traditional method of analysis does not allow an identification of the structural relationships involved in the determination of expenditures. In other words, the analysis of the reduced form equations employed in most of these studies masks interrelationships among the variables, usually making it impossible to separate the demand and supply influences on expenditures.[c] For example, a significantly positive coefficient for the income variable using a reduced form equation could suggest either that the increased expenditure resulted from an increased willingness or ability to purchase public goods (demand) or merely the ability of public employees to obtain a share of the added income of the community through higher wages.

Secondly, this analysis of reduced form equations often makes policy conclusions difficult if not impossible to obtain. For example, a significantly positive coefficient for the aid variable could result from an actual increase in governmental services due to increased employment or an increased cost of providing the same services due to wage increases gained by employees. The policy recommendation obviously depends upon which effect is predominant.

Thirdly, the traditional form of determinant analysis and the conclusions derived therefrom are of little help in forecasting expenditures for a particular city government. Because of the aggregative nature of analysis employed in many determinants studies, it is not possible to predict growth in the various components of expenditure beyond a function by function level. However, it is often that forecasts of some of these components (for example, payrolls) rather than total expenditures which is of most interest to policymakers.

Over roughly the same period, a related although much less voluminous body of literature has evolved forcusing upon the determinants of local (and state) public employment.[d] In some of these studies—Fabricant (21), Manvel (42) and Horowitz (34)—public employment was analyzed along with public expenditure, although no attempt was made to link the determinants of each in a comprehensive theory. In others—Ehrenberg (18) and (19)—the demand for public employees was estimated after the employment budget (not total expenditure) was

---

[a]No attempt to list them will be made here. However, for reviews of these studies see Bahl (3), Barlow (9), Bird (13), and Wilensky (68). More recent studies include Borcherding and Deacon (16) and Bergstrom and Goodman (12).

[b]For an excellent critique of this literature, see Elliot Morss (44).

[c]For some of the few attempts at such a distinction, see Miner (43) and McMahon (41).

[d]See Fabricant (21), Manvel (42), Horowitz (34), Landon and Baird (39) and Ehrenberg (18) (19).

assumed to be determined. Further, in the former studies, no attempt was made to measure the impact of public wages on public employment, while in neither group of studies was the effect of public employment changes on public expenditures considered.

Still a further body of literature has recently evolved relating to the determinants of public employee wages.[e] However, in these studies, the interrelationships between public employment and public wage determination have often been ignored. Further, no attempt has been made to estimate the effect of wage rate changes on public expenditure.

In summary, the three groups of literature cited above have existed in relative isolation of one another, with few attempts being undertaken to integrate their implications. Clearly what is needed is a comprehensive model which synthesizes the important elements of each approach.

Scope of the Present Analysis

It is a major contention of this study that all of these criticisms result from the inability of the traditional models to explain the process by which the determinants affect the level of total expenditures as well as its wage, employment, and nonpayroll cost components. The explanation of this process would add greatly to the understanding of governmental expenditure decisions, enable more accurate policy prescriptions to be suggested, and make predictions of future expenditure levels for particular cities more reliable. In fact, without a clearer understanding than now exists of how particular determinants affect expenditure levels, further analysis of the determinants of public expenditure (or wage rates and employment levels for that matter) proceeds on extremely tenuous theoretical grounds.

The purpose of this study, then, is to derive and test a model which is capable of explaining that process of expenditure determination. The model specifies, in some detail, the effects of the determinants on the various components of total expenditures—wage rates, employment levels, and nonpayroll costs. The test involves the application of the model both to explain public expenditure variation for a cross-section of U.S. cities, and to analyze time-series growth in expenditures for a particular city.

The reason for employing this model to explain both cross-sectional and time-series variation should be emphasized. In the former case, the attempt is to determine the factors that underlie expenditure variation among cities while in the latter case, the desire is to explain expenditure growth for a particular city. It should be recognized that the results obtained through either analysis separately do not allow one to imply what the other results might show. Therefore, since the desire here is to understand both relationships among

---

[e]See Schmenner (56), Thornton (63) and Kasper (36).

expenditure levels among cities and within a particular city, cross-sectional as well as time-series analysis is required.

The study is divided into five chapters. The remainder of this chapter is devoted to a brief discussion of the major findings of this study. In Chapter 2, the assumptions and statistical form of the general model are presented in detail. Chapter 3 includes a test of the model on aggregate cross-section data for thirty-nine U.S. cities. In Chapter 4, the application of the model to an analysis of the expenditure growth in New York City is demonstrated. Chapter 5 focuses on the significance of the results derived from both cross-sectional and time series analysis, as well as suggestions for future research.

Summary of Major Conclusions

The model employed in this study divides current expenditures into payroll and nonpayroll costs, and payroll costs into employment levels and average wage rates. Wage and employment levels (and therefore payroll costs) of labor are then determined in a demand and supply model of public employment, with labor employment and the general price level determining nonpayroll costs.

The use of the model to explain cross-sectional variation in expenditures of thirty-nine city governments suggests several important conclusions regarding the expenditure determination process. First, the opportunity (private-sector) wage was the most significant determinant of public-sector wages, indicating the possibility of wage rollout from the private to the public sector. Second, the service workload was the most significant determinant of employment levels, suggesting the responsiveness of public officials to variations in service conditions. Finally, it was suggested that the significance of income and aid in previous studies probably has resulted from the former's effect on wages and the latter's effect on employment.

Similarly, the time-series analysis of six New York City government functions yielded some interesting conclusions regarding historical growth in expenditures. First, for police, fire, and environmental protection, real wage growth accounted for greater proportions of payroll cost growth than did employment growth, while for social services, public schools, and higher education the reverse was the case. Second, real wage growth was more important than employment growth in producing payroll cost increases for uniformed-delivery personnel while the reverse was true for nonuniformed-nondelivery personnel. Thirdly, for most functions, price increases accounted for roughly twice the amount of nonpayroll cost growth that was accounted for by employment growth.

Finally, the elasticities estimated from both the cross-sectional and time-series analyses suggest some cause for alarm concerning the severity of the municipal fiscal crisis. Specifically, the results suggest a wage inelastic demand curve for labor as well as a wage and employment elastic public expenditure function. Taken together, these findings suggest reasons for concern for the ability of municipalities to solve their own fiscal problems.

2 A Public Employment Model of Municipal Expenditure Determination

It has been argued above that a major criticism of the determinants studies concerns their inability to explain the process by which these traditional determinants affect expenditures. The purpose here is to detail an alternative model applicable to both cross-sectional and time-series analysis, which specifies these interrelationships so often masked in previous studies. To this end, that which follows centers, in turn, around: a discussion of the importance of each of the basic assumptions of this model; a specification of the structural form of all of its equations; and an investigation of the relationship between variables specified in this model and those of the traditional determinants studies.

The Basic Assumptions of the Model

In simple form, the model is based upon five assumptions.

1. The city government produces services of homogeneous quality with two homogeneous factors of production: labor and nonlabor.
2. The services are produced through a process governed by a fixed proportions production function with labor as a limitational factor (that is, increased labor is a necessary but not sufficient condition for increased output).
3. The price of labor inputs (wage rates)[a] is affected by the quantity of these inputs employed.
4. The city can purchase any quantity of nonlabor inputs without affecting their prices.
5. Cost minimizing city officials translate citizen preferences for public output into a corresponding demand function for public employment.

At this point, it is necessary to analyze the importance of each of the above assumptions in the functioning of the entire model. The function of the first assumption—that of two homogeneous inputs—is to provide simplicity. More specifically, the assumption rules out any substitutability in production among types of labor or nonlabor inputs.

The second assumption, detailing the character of the production function, is required in order to draw a direct link between employment of labor and

---

[a]Wage rates used in this chapter refers to all forms of compensation including pension contributions, health insurance benefits, and so forth.

11

nonlabor inputs. Although in the real world there are certainly exceptions (highway construction, for example), many areas of city government output, because of their service nature rely heavily on labor inputs and allow little chance for capital substitution. Further, to the extent that the predominant form of nonlabor inputs is comprised of the materials and supplies directly used by employees to produce the service, the assumption of a fixed proportions production function with labor as limitational has added legitimacy.

The third assumption concerns the determination of public employee wages. Because the city demands some workers with somewhat specialized skills (for example, policemen, firemen, teachers) and oftentimes employs a significant portion of the total urban labor force, it seems necessary that an upward sloping rather than a perfectly elastic labor supply function be incorporated into the model.

The fourth assumption relates to prices that the city must pay in order to purchase nonlabor inputs from the private sector. The assumption made here is that the city acts like a competitive firm and purchases all the nonlabor inputs it needs at the going price. While it would be possible to hypothesize that prices and quantities of nonlabor inputs were jointly determined, the added complexity introduced into the model as a result of this assumption does not appear to be warranted, especially given the aggregate nature of the data available for testing.

The final assumption is that the city translates citizen public service preferences into a demand function for public employees, assuming cost minimization. The importance of this assumption is twofold. First, the city is assumed to act merely to reflect citizen preferences, not to determine them, and to be able to determine an appropriate level of public output, and hence employment, to satisfy these preferences. Secondly, the cost minimization assumption is necessary so that the employment level is uniquely determined by the desired level of output. Without this assumption, the appropriate level of output could be obtained by hiring more than the minimum number of employees necessary, with the result that a unique level of employment could not be determined.

The process of expenditure determination, given these assumptions, can then be easily described. Wage rates and employment levels of labor are determined through the interaction of their demand and supply curves. Then, the dictates of the production function determine the nonlabor input, given the level of labor employment. Finally, the city's expenditure is determined as the sum of the products of these quantities of the labor and nonlabor inputs and their corresponding prices—the bargained for wage rate for employees, and the market determined price level for nonlabor inputs.

In sum, the purpose here has been to define the assumptions of a model meant to explain the process of city government expenditure determination. The focus of the discussion will now turn to the specification of the structural form of each of the equations in the model.

The Structural Form of the Model

The basic model is composed of the following five equations:

$$\hat{W}^i = f(A_1^i) \tag{2.1}$$

$$\hat{E}_p^i = f(A_2^i) \tag{2.2}$$

$$\hat{NC}_p^i = f(A_3^i) \tag{2.3}$$

$$\hat{LC}_p^i \equiv \hat{W} \cdot \hat{E}_p^i \tag{2.4}$$

$$\hat{X}_p^i \equiv \hat{LC}_p^i + \hat{NC}_p^i \tag{2.5}$$

where:

W^i = public-sector wage rates in function i

E_p^i = public-sector employment per 1000 population in function i

NC_p^i = nonpayroll costs per 1000 population in function i

LC_p^i = payroll costs per 1000 population in function i

X_p^i = public expenditure per 1000 population in function i

A_1^i = determinants of public employee wages in function i

A_2^i = determinants of public-sector employment in function i

A_3^i = determinants of nonpayroll expenditures in function i

$\hat{}$ = estimated value

The task of this section is to define those variables which might be considered determinants of wages (A_1^i), employment (A_2^i) and nonpayroll expenditures (A_3^i), as well as the process by which these determinants have their effects.

The concept of wage rollout is basic to the determination of wages in Equation (2.1). Applying Wilbur Thompson's argument (62) to the public sector, the greater the private-sector wage, the higher will be public-sector wages. The process involved in this relationship results from the interaction of two forces. First, competition between public and private sectors in the hiring of similar workers will have a tendency to erase wage differentials—workers leaving lower paying jobs, and moving to higher paying ones. Secondly, a demonstration effect, arising out of union competition will have a similar effect—wage increases won in the private sector will encourage public employees to demand similar increases. Hence the formulation of the wage equation hypothesizes a positive relationship between the private-sector wage rate (the opportunity wage) and that in the public sector.

Another concept important to wage determination is labor mobility. Thompson (62) argues that the greater the mobility of labor between sectors, the greater the amount of the wage rollout. The process by which mobility influences wage rates can be described in terms of either a competition effect or a demonstration effect. In the former case, labor immobility prevents workers from leaving lower paying jobs to accept higher paying ones, thus preventing the shifts in labor supply which tend to eliminate wage differentials. In the latter case, the possibility of obtaining higher pay elsewhere can be seen as adding to union unwillingness to settle for less than has been demonstrated to be obtainable. It should be recognized, however, that mobility is more important in the competitive than in the union case.

Applying this argument more specifically to the case at hand, the greater the mobility of public employees into the private sector, the more closely will their wages reflect those in the private sector. Given the typical stability of government employment, it is assumed that public employees will be paid lower wages than their private-sector counterparts. The mobility variable is thus hypothesized to be positively related to public-sector wages, because the more easily public employees can obtain private-sector employment, the higher will be their wages. One factor adding to the immobility of public employees into the private sector is the increasing importance of city contributions to pension funds, which can have the effect of locking a worker into his job.

Other important determinants relate to both the ability of the city to finance as well as the ability of union leaders to obtain wage rate increases. Eckstein and Wilson (69) have argued and shown empirically that both industry profits and the extent of unionization are positively related to private-sector wage rates. In the case of industry profits, the process involves the argument that profits represent the ability of businesses to finance wage increases without raising product price and thereby affecting product demand. In the case of union power, the process involves the ability of union leaders to extract wage increases from management. Applying such an argument to the public sector, it follows that the greater the fiscal capacity of the city (that is, the ability of the citizens to finance wage increases), as well as the union power of employees (that is, the ability of employees to dictate contract terms), the higher will be public-employee wages.

Before proceeding, it should be pointed out that the concept of fiscal capacity as used here is comprised of two components—internal and external access to funds. The greater the capacity to finance wage increases from either source, the higher will be public wages. Further, it might be argued that, at least at the margin, increased external access could have more effect on wages than increased internal access to funds. This effect could certainly result from the actions of city officials who, for political reasons, might seem more frugal with funds obtained locally than with those obtained elsewhere.

The hypothesis of any relationship between employment and wage rates in the wage equation is closely dependent upon the assumption of union existence and behavior. First, if no union exists, and the city hires such a small number of the area labor force so as not to affect wage rates, the city acts like a competitive firm and takes the wage rate as given. Under these conditions, no relationship would exist between wage rates and employment levels. Second, if unions exist but bargain only for wages and will provide any number of workers at the bargained for wage rate, then there should likewise be no relationship between employment and wages in the wage equation. Finally, if due to a shortage of workers, union officials agreed to recruit more members in return for higher wages, or if the city hired so many employees as to affect area wage rates, then there could be a positive relationship hypothesized between the variables. While each of these explanations might appear plausible on a priori grounds, this determination is left to the empirical chapters.

In addition to the factors mentioned to this point, it is possible to conceive of purely regional (in the case of cross-sectional analysis) or temporal (in the case of time-series analysis) determinants of wage rates. For instance, because of an aversion to public-sector employment, workers of a particular region or at a particular point of time might, ceteris paribus, demand higher wages than public employees in another region or time. The converse might also be the case in a region or time where these workers were held in high esteem. These and other such purely regional or temporal phenomena could affect wage rates through a process completely different from those of the variables described above, and therefore, need to be explicitly taken into account in the specification of the wage equation.

A primary determinant of employment in Equation (2.2) is the need for the service on the part of the citizenry. To use an example, it might be expected that as the amount of crime in a city increases, there would be a similar increase in the demand for policemen. The process involved here is simple to explain, being based upon an assumption of fixed technology as well as the existence of a production function exhibiting both fixed proportions and constant returns to scale. On the one hand, increased crime might cause citizens to perceive that their probability of being victimized has increased thereby causing them to demand added policemen to combat the trend. On the other hand, increased crime (particularly of a violent nature) might cause policemen to demand additional employment for their own protection (two-man patrol cars rather than one, for example).

It should also be recognized that this effect certainly exists in other city departments, among them fire and sanitation. In each case, increased service needs by the citizenry might result in an increased demand for public employees. Sacks (53) and others have hypothesized such a relationship in the case of public schools between expenditures and pupils, although none have suggested a similar relationship to explain employment in such functions as police and fire.

Another factor which certainly would influence the demand for public employees relates to the number of nonresidents who frequent the city. The argument involved here suggests that the greater the demands of nonresidents for city services, the larger will be public-employment levels. Nonresidents who visit the city represent a drain on city services in the form of traffic congestion, additional fire hazards, and so forth. The resulting dilution of the effectiveness of the service might cause city residents to demand more employees to improve services for personal reasons, or city merchants to do likewise to add to the attractiveness of the downtown area to entice more suburbanites to their stores. Whatever the specifics of the process, however, it seems clear that the greater the nonresident component, the greater will be the demand for public employees. Both Bahl (2) and Brazer (17) found such a variable to be a significant determinant of per capita expenditures, but neither considered it as a determinant of public employment.

As in the case of the wage equation, the fiscal capacity of the citizenry is hypothesized here to be positively related to employment levels. Specifically, the greater the capacity to finance city expenditures, the greater will be the resulting level of public employment. It should be emphasized, however, that this argument (whether applied to the wage or employment equation) should not be confused with the relatively meaningless hypothesis that revenues determine expenditures (or vice versa). Rather, the concept of fiscal capacity used here can be viewed as a sort of budget constraint which limits the ability of the city to grant wage increases or hire additional employees. According to this interpretation, the city seeks to maximize some citizen utility function subject to the constraint placed upon it by its access to funds both internal and external (that is, fiscal capacity). Although not always explained in these terms, the inclusion of per capita income and aid variables in the traditional determinants studies might be viewed as a sort of budget constraint, measuring the ability of a locality to purchase public services.

A further variable which certainly affects employment is wage rates. The argument here is that wage rates and employment levels are inversely related. The process through which wage rates have their effect can be simply explained. An inverse relationship between wages and employment demands is consistent with the existence of a city government budget constraint. Under these conditions, the granting of increased wages to public employees would lessen the amount of money available to the city for hiring new employees. In other words, in regions or points in time when wage rates were high, ceteris paribus, employment levels would be low.

As in the case of the wage equation, it is possible that regional (cross-section) or temporal (time-series) differences might affect employment through a process divorced from that of the other variables considered. For example, employment in one region (or time period) may be higher than in another region (or time) simply because there was a desire on the part of the citizens or city officials in the region to keep the unemployed "off the streets." Because of the possibility of such differences, these variables have been included in the model.

In the final equation, nonpayroll costs are hypothesized to be affected by three factors. First, employment levels are assumed positively related to nonpayroll costs. This relationship results from the assumption of a fixed proportions production function with labor as a limitational factor. Secondly, the average price level of nonlabor inputs is hypothesized to be positively related to nonpayroll costs. Third, the possibility of distinct regional or temporal differences in nonpayroll costs (apart from the price or employment variables) is accounted for by the inclusion here of such variables.

The basic model, as described above, then, is made up of the following five equations:

$$\hat{W}^i = f(W_O, F, M, U, \hat{E}_p^i, I) \tag{2.6}$$

$$\hat{E}_p^i = f(\hat{W}^i, S_p^i, F, C, I) \tag{2.7}$$

$$N\hat{C}_p^i = f(E_p^i, P^i, I) \tag{2.8}$$

$$L\hat{C}_p^i \equiv \hat{W}^i \cdot \hat{E}_p^i \tag{2.9}$$

$$\hat{X}_p^i \equiv L\hat{C}_p^i + N\hat{C}_p^i \tag{2.10}$$

where:

W^i = public-sector wage in function i

W_O = opportunity wage in the private sector

F = fiscal capacity of citizens

M = mobility of public employees into the private sector

U = unionization of public employees

I = regional or temporal influences

S_p^i = service needs of population per 1000 population in function i

C = centralization of population within the SMSA

P^i = price level of nonlabor inputs in function i

E_p^i = public employment per 1000 population in function i

NC_p^i = nonpayroll costs per 1000 population in function i

LC_p^i = payroll costs per 1000 population in function i

X_p^i = current expenditures per 1000 population in function i

$\hat{}$ = estimated value

This formulation can immediately be seen as simply a demand and supply model. In the labor market, demand as indicated by the employment equation, and supply represented by the wage equation determine employment and wage rates. When the coefficient of employment (E_p) in the wage equation is zero, the model describes a labor market characterized by a perfectly elastic supply curve. When the coefficients of both unionization (U) and employment (E_p) are zero, the model describes the labor market situation for a particular firm in a competitive market. In the nonlabor market, demand and supply determine nonpayroll costs. More specifically, nonlabor demand is determined by the employment of labor (because of an assumed fixed proportions production function) while nonlabor prices are determined outside the model by market forces beyond the control of the city. Expenditures are then determined by the sum of payroll costs (LC_p) and nonpayroll costs (NC_p) and, therefore, indirectly as a result of the interaction of these labor demand and supply influences.

Relation of the Model and
Determinants Studies

As indicated previously, the difficulties in separating demand and supply effects upon expenditures are well known. As a result, Roy Bahl (2) has suggested that the determinants variables can be placed into three categories: income and wealth variables, and capacity to finance variables.

Income and wealth variables are supposed to measure the effect of the willingness and ability of citizens to purchase public goods as well as the need of those citizens for public goods. Median family income and per capita retail sales fall in the first category while fraction of the population with incomes below $3,000, and percentage nonwhite falls into the second.

Demographic variables measure both the overall size of the population demanding services and the distribution of the population as it affects the ease of providing government services. The size of the nonresident population is often chosen for the latter.

Finally, capacity to finance variables proxy the ability of the citizens, through external and internal means, to purchase public goods. Some measure of federal and state aid is usually chosen as a proxy for access to external financing, while median housing values or per capita assessed values are often used to measure internal resources.

It should be recognized that each of these three categories of variables has been incorporated into the alternative model, either through their inclusion in the wage equation, the employment equation, or in both wage and employment equations. Specifically, income and wealth variables have been included in both equations. In the wage equation these factors indicate both the ability of the community to pay wages to its public employees and a reflection of the demands of public employees for wages commensurate with the standard of living enjoyed by the citizens of the community. In the employment equation, income and wealth variables serve as indicators of the willingness and ability of the citizenry to purchase public goods (thereby demanding public employees) as well as measures of need by certain segments of the population for those services. Similarly, capacity to finance variables also enter both wage and employment equations. The ability to finance affects the wage settlements of public employees as well as the demand for public employees.

On the other hand, demographic variables directly enter only the employ-ment equation. For example, the distribution of the population within the SMSA, and the size of the nonresident population both determine the demand for government workers. However, any link to the wage equation would have to be based upon the argument that city population characteristics affect public employee demands for wages directly rather than through an indirect effect on private-sector wages. The exclusion of the demographic variables from the wage equation was based upon the argument that these factors affect the general level of wages in the city rather than public employee wages specifically.

It should be evident, at this point, that the traditional determinants are included in this alternative model of the process of public expenditure determi-nation. However, the primary distinction between these two approaches is that the model described here seeks to uncover the behavioral relationships which underlie the process of expenditure determination, while the traditional ap-proach seeks only to determine the net effect of each of the sets of variables on the level of total expenditures, wages, or employment.

3 Interurban Variations in City Government Expenditures

In previous chapters, the limitations of past determinants studies have been described and an alternative model of the process of expenditure determination suggested. The task of the present chapter is to test the ability of the model to explain interurban variations in the level of city government expenditure for police, fire, and the common functions[a] for 1966 and 1971 and to compare these cross-sectional estimates. Accordingly, the empirical specification of the variables in the model will be presented first, followed by an analysis of the distributions of the dependent and independent variables. At that point the actual regression results will be discussed and finally, their significance assessed.

Empirical Specification of the Cross-Section Model

The testing of the model described previously requires the estimation of three equations:

$$\hat{W}^i = f(W_O, F, U, M, \hat{E}^i_p, R) \tag{3.1}$$

$$\hat{E}^i_p = f(S^i_p, C, F, \hat{W}^i, R) \tag{3.2}$$

$$N\hat{C}^i_p = f(P, E^i_p, R) \tag{3.3}$$

where:

W_O = opportunity wage of public employees

F = fiscal capacity of citizens

U = extent of unionization

M = mobility of public employees into the private sector

S^i_p = service need of citizens per 1000 population

---

[a]The common functions as defined by the Bureau of the Census include police, fire, sanitation and sewerage, libraries, parks and recreation, highways, water supply, financial administration, and general control.

21

C = centralization of population within the SMSA

P = market-determined price of nonlabor goods

R = regional characteristics

However, before it is possible to begin the test, it is necessary to describe the specific hypotheses to be tested, as well as the proxies chosen to measure each of these variables.[b]

As suggested in the previous chapter, each of the independent variables in the wage equation is hypothesized to be positively correlated with public-employee wages. In related studies, Eckstein and Wilson (69) found unemployment (labor mobility) and unionization to be significant determinants of private-sector wage rates. Schmenner (56) reported the opportunity wage and extent of unionization to be significant determinants of wages of police, fire, and common function employees. Thornton (63) also determined that unionization was a significant factor in explaining wage rates of teachers, while Kasper (36) found that per capita income was the most important determinant of teacher salaries.

For the purposes of this study, average wages of policemen, firemen, and all common function employees were used as the dependent variable in the wage equation.[c,d] As a measure of the opportunity wage, average earnings of private-sector service employees (as obtained from *County Business Patterns*, U.S. Department of Commerce) was chosen. For the fiscal capacity of the city, median family income[e] was selected as a measure of internal capacity, while federal and state aid as a percentage of general revenue was employed as an estimate of the dependence of the locality on external aid. The mobility of public-sector employees was proxied by the area unemployment rate, while the extent of public-sector unionization was measured by the fraction of the

---

[b]A key to the regression variables is shown in Appendix A, while the specific sources of each of the measures of these variables can be found in Appendix B.

[c]Average wages were simply obtained by dividing payrolls by the number of full-time equivalent employees. Included in payrolls are wages and salaries as well as overtime pay, before deduction of taxes, health insurance, and so forth. More detailed data published by the Bureau of Labor Statistics could not be used because these figures did not cover all city government employees. Such coverage is necessary to enable a comparison with published expenditure figures.

[d]While the choice of these three functions lessens the possibility of variations due to differing functional responsibility among cities, this problem is not eliminated. For example, the existence of special fire districts overlying city limits could lessen the responsibility of fire departments in some cities. Further, in some cities separate police forces, for example, transit police or county sheriffs, might lessen the need for city policemen. Finally, there is almost certainly some variation in functional responsibility (perhaps shared responsibility with another level of government) in other common functions such as libraries, parks and recreation, and sanitation. These possibilities should be kept in mind when interpreting the results that follow.

[e]While fiscal capacity might be better estimated by use of the property tax base or some other such variable, income was chosen to enable a comparison with past studies.

private-sector labor force in the states that were union members. (The level of private-sector unionization was chosen here because of the lack of adequate data on public employee unions.) In addition, regional dummies for the four census regions were used to detect the existence of distinct regional characteristics.[f]

Of the variables in the employment equation, service needs and fiscal capacity were hypothesized to be positively correlated with employment levels, while centralization of the population and the public employee average wage are posited as negatively related. In similar studies of per capita expenditures, Fisher (23) found per capita income and aid (fiscal capacity) to be significant determinants on the state and local level. Both Brazer (17) and Bahl (2) found median family income and aid (fiscal capacity) as well as the fraction of the SMSA population residing in the city (centralization) to be significant expenditure determinants although Bahl (2) measured the aid variable as a fraction of general revenues, while Brazer (17) specified aid in per capita terms. In addition to income and aid, Sacks (53) and Sacks and Harris (54) identified the enrollment ratio (service need) as an important determinant of educational expenditures. Finally, Horowitz (34) found both income and aid to be significant determinants of state and local government employment as well as expenditures.

For estimational purposes, full-time equivalent numbers of employees for police, fire, and the common functions were used as measures of employment. As in the wage equations, the fiscal capacity was measured by median family income and the fraction of the city's revenues which were derived from federal and state aid. The centralization of the population was estimated by the fraction of the SMSA population residing inside the central city. Regional dummies for the four census regions were employed to detect distinct regional characteristics. The service need of the citizens for police was proxied by the number of felonies per 1000 population, for fire by the number of fires per 1000 population, and for all the common functions by the number of fires and felonies combined per 1000 population.[g] The same measure of wages as specified in the wage setting equation was used for the employment equation.

In accordance with the arguments set forth in the preceding chapter, both independent variables in the nonpayroll cost equation are hypothesized to be positively correlated with the dependent variable. Since no similar division of expenditures into payroll and nonpayroll components has been attempted, it is not possible to cite results of previous studies which apply here.

For the purpose of this study, the level of nonpayroll costs was estimated by the difference between current expenditures and labor costs (wages times

---

[f]In the equations, the dummies for the central, west, and southern regions were employed, so that the results indicate differences in the regions from the east. For a description of this use of dummies, see Suits (60).

[g]Ideally, measures of service need for the other common functions (e.g., rubbish collections, library visits, etc.) should be included here. However, data unavailability limits this proxy to police and fire measures.

employment) for each function.[h] The price of nonlabor inputs was estimated by the cost of living for a family of four for an intermediate budget as reported by the Bureau of Labor Statistics.[i] In addition, the same estimates as described above were used to measure employment characteristics and the existence of regional characteristics.

The sample of cities used to test the model is comprised of the thirty-nine U.S. cities presented in Table 3-1. In 1970, these cities ranged in population from about 60,000 in both Lancaster, Pennsylvania and Portland, Maine to the almost 8 million population in New York City. It should be noted that the choice of these cities was based upon the availability of data and therefore does not represent a random sample. The basic data constraint was formed by the limited availability of the nonlabor price data necessary to estimate the nonpayroll cost equation, although several other cities had to be omitted because of a lack of adequate public-sector wage or employment data. Still, the sample includes cities with populations fairly evenly distributed among the various size classes. Specifically, in 1970 six had population of more than 1 million, thirteen had populations of between 50,000 and 1 million, ten had populations of between 250,000 and 500,000, while ten had populations below 250,000.[j]

Before proceeding, it would be helpful to spell out in detail the alternative forms of this basic model which were fitted. The difference between these cases stems only from specifications of the wage equation. Specifically, the two cases assume the following form of the wage equation:

Case I:

$$\hat{W}^i = f(W_o, F, U, M, R) \tag{3.4A}$$

Case II:

$$\hat{W}^i = f(W_o, F, M, U, R, \hat{E}_p) \tag{3.4B}$$

---

[h]Nonpayroll costs include all other expenditures. Included in this list are materials, supplies, pension costs, debt service, and so forth. Further, while capital expenditures were excluded from highways and sanitation expenditures, such was not possible for the other functions. Due to the aggregate nature of the data, it was not possible to treat each of these items separately.

[i]The obvious weakness in this measure is that some of the items used in the calculation of this cost of living are not purchased by city governments (e.g., entertainment, and federal taxes) while some things purchased by the city are excluded (e.g., office supplies and maintenance equipment). The reason for the choice was that this series covered a wider range of cities than the consumer price index or wholesale price index. In any event, the assumption made here is that variation in the cost of nonlabor inputs purchased by cities were roughly comparable to increase in the cost of living faced by its citizens.

[j]It should be noted here, that six of the cities in the sample included in the west region are located in California. This fact should be kept in mind when interpreting the results of the following regressions with respect to this region.

Table 3-1
The Structure of Population in the Thirty-Nine City Sample—1970

East	1970 Population
Boston	641,071
Buffalo	462,768
Hartford	158,017
Lancaster	57,690
New York	7,895,563
Philadelphia	1,949,996
Pittsburgh	520,117
Portland	65,116
Central	
Cedar Rapids	110,652
Chicago	3,369,357
Gary	175,415
Cincinnati	451,455
Cleveland	750,879
Dayton	242,917
Detroit	1,513,601
Kansas City, Kansas	168,213
Kansas City, Missouri	507,330
Milwaukee	717,372
Minneapolis	434,400
St. Paul	309,714
St. Louis	622,236
Wichita	276,554
South	
Atlanta	496,973
Austin	251,808
Baltimore	905,787
Baton Rouge	271,922
Dallas	844,401
Durham	95,438
Houston	1,232,802
Orlando	99,006
Washington	756,510
West	
Bakersfield	69,515
Denver	514,678

Table 3-1 (cont.)

West	1970 Population
Long Beach	358,879
Los Angeles	2,809,813
Oakland	361,561
San Diego	697,027
San Francisco	715,674
Seattle	530,831

Source: *1970 Census of Population*, U.S. Department of Commerce.

Case I, then, assumes the wage decision is made independently of a consideration of employment, while Case II assumes that the wage and employment decisions are made simultaneously.

For case I, Equations (3.1) and (3.3) were fited using ordinary least squares (OLS), while Equation (3.2) was fitted using the estimated values of wages (W) obtained from Equation (3.1) rather than observed values. The reason for using estimated values of wages (rather than observed ones) was to lessen the problem of simultaneous equation bias, arising from possible effects of employment on wages. In Case II, such a technique (two stage least squares) was used to fit both Equations (3.1) and (3.2), while ordinary least squares was employed for estimating Equation (3.3). Finally, all equations were fitted in linear terms. This choice was based upon the fact that there appeared no a priori justification for the alternative specification.

The Distribution of Dependent and Independent Variables

Before presenting the results comprising the test of the model, it is informative to investigate the distribution of the variables in order to determine their relative size and variability. Table 3-2 presents the means, standard deviations, and coefficients of variation of each of the dependent and independent variables for the two years under analysis—1966 and 1971. Worthy of specific note is the existence of the relatively larger coefficients of variation for the employment variables than for the wage variables, and for nonpayroll costs than for expenditures. These coefficients would indicate that there is more to explain in terms of variation for employment and nonpayroll costs than for the other two variables. It should also be noted that no particular pattern exists in the variation is evident when comparing 1966 and 1971 coefficients of variation for each variable.

The intercorrelation matrix in Table 3-3 allows two determinations to be

Table 3-2

Means, Standard Deviation, and Coefficients of Variation of Variables in the Model, 1966 and 1971

	1966			1971		
	Mean	Standard Deviation	Coefficient of Variation	Mean	Standard Deviation	Coefficient of Variation
WP	7102.8	1064.9	14.99	9722.9	1475.7	15.17
WF	7221.1	1262.8	17.48	10,121.1	1874.0	18.51
WC	6642.4	1268.5	19.09	9588.7	1690.8	17.63
EPP	2.4969	0.9084	36.38	3.1534	1.2621	40.02
EFP	1.7286	0.5201	30.08	1.8952	0.6180	32.60
ECP	9.5987	2.2690	23.63	10.9144	2.8854	26.43
SERV	4025.0	631.2	15.68	5557.7	737.7	13.27
AIDP	19.7846	10.7673	54.42	26.2730	13.4101	51.04
UNION	27.7692	8.9660	32.28	27.7692	8.9660	32.28
CEN	40.6404	19.8224	48.77	37.7886	20.9182	55.35
FELP	28.5383	9.4683	33.17	51.4904	16.6876	32.40
FIRP	10.9184	4.9953	45.75	13.6800	5.3028	39.76
NEED	39.4567	11.0596	28.02	65.1704	18.5918	28.52
NLP	4169.6	3058.3	73.35	14,858.9	12,866.5	86.59
NLF	2607.1	2543.6	97.56	6574.5	4173.3	63.48
NLC	25,484.0	11,030.3	43.28	50,581.9	39,365.8	77.83
COST	9210.5	512.4	5.56	10,925.1	740.3	6.78
INC	8276.3	689.1	8.32	10,424.7	888.7	8.52
UNEM	2.8308	0.8320	29.39	5.2692	2.0285	38.49
XPP	22,222	8988	40.45	46,313	27,654	59.71
XFP	15,013	5234	34.86	25,545	8902	34.85
XCP	89,106	23,434	26.30	155,367	66,395	42.73

Note: See Appendix A for a key to the variables and Appendix B for their sources.

made. First, a rough approximation of the relative importance of the determinants in explaining variation in the dependent variables can be obtained by comparing their simple correlation coefficients. Secondly, the existence of problems of multicollinearity arising out of intercorrelation of the independent variables can be determined by examining the respective correlation coefficients.

With regard to the relative explanatory power of the determinants, several conclusions can be drawn. For the wage setting equation, particularly noteworthy is the high simple correlation between the opportunity wage (*SERV*) and that of police, fire, and common function employees (*WP, WF,* and *WC* respectively). In the employment equation, relatively large correlations were

Table 3-3A
An Intercorrelation Matrix of the Regression Variables: 1966

	WF1	WC1	EPP1	EFP1	ECP1	SERV1	AIDP1	UNION	UNEM1	CEN1	FELP1	FIRP1	NEED1	NLP1	NLF1	NLC1	COST1	SOUTH	WEST	CENT	XPP1	XFP1	XCP1	INC1
WP1	8705	7976	3365	0135	2474	7766	2591	4583	2664	-2902	4358	-1109	3230	0922	-1236	1346	5833	-2879	3222	-0614	5742	3023	6362	4442
WF1		8756	1651	-1189	0290	7769	1646	5105	3338	-3785	5155	-2218	3411	3376	0322	2485	5789	-4103	6150	-0508	4807	3467	5786	6471
WC1			1570	0189	-0486	6903	1301	5339	3561	-3598	4294	-0953	3246	3374	1559	0803	6287	-5343	5998	0476	4504	4456	5354	6466
EPP1				3628	7782	3633	4667	4108	0580	-0472	3859	3654	4954	1753	-0332	0754	2915	-0246	-1912	-0817	9000	3294	6235	-1503
EFP1					4166	0050	3843	0596	1451	-2938	-0009	5853	2635	0237	2741	-0185	3655	1018	-1575	-1117	2791	7712	2714	-2938
ECP1						2513	3401	1408	-0843	3100	-0845	3278	4134	0746	-0312	1788	2374	-2514	-2736	-2209	6907	3169	6948	-3747
SERV1							1200	2935	4988	-2949	5659	-0389	4669	3930	0918	1471	4943	-1500	4925	2437	6391	5941	3749	3764
AIDP1								3175	-0185	-1358	0727	0554	0873	-2404	-1186	0837	4454	-2453	-0618	-0306	3479	2908	3346	0024
UNION									-0166	-3826	1826	-0681	1255	1772	-1173	0857	4953	-6678	1531	2834	4732	1920	4106	3412
UNEM1										-0804	2518	1601	2878	3594	4259	0894	1491	-1539	5608	-3339	2271	4039	1569	0248
CEN1											-2615	-0879	-2636	-3507	-1906	-2183	-3638	4053	-2684	-0310	-2042	-4543	-3183	-0028
FELP1												0815	8929	3697	1391	0643	1870	0173	2445	-0239	5447	3001	4523	1802
FIRP1													5214	0200	0965	-0608	2491	-0915	-1510	-0223	2323	3265	1249	-3917
NEED1														3256	1627	0276	2726	-0264	1411	-0305	5712	4437	4044	-0226
NLP1															6079	5408	0501	-0289	5202	-2567	4739	4565	4437	1376
NLF1																3718	-0919	0164	3615	-2433	1456	6582	2275	0432
NLC1																	0793	1076	3313	-3025	2756	5932	2672	1188
COST1																		-6898	2643	0899	4039	4444	4381	4277
SOUTH																			-2782	-4098	-0839	-2386	-0756	-4200
WEST																				-3801	1030	3324	2838	5174
CENT																					-1795	-2921	-2772	2097
XPP1																						4904	8119	0584
XFP1																							5592	0811
XCP1																								1632

Table 3-3B
An Intercorrelation Matrix of the Regression Variables: 1971

	WF2	WC2	EPP2	EFP2	ECP2	SERV2	AIDP2	UNION	UNEM2	CEN2	FELP2	FIRP2	NEED2	NLP2	NLF2	NLC2	COST2	SOUTH	WEST	CENT	XPP2	XFP2	XCP2	INC2
WP2	8514	8604	4374	-0311	1972	7612	2222	5206	1564	-3143	4283	0477	3980	3753	4716	3244	5253	-2588	3759	-1468	5604	5526	5227	4316
WF2		8536	2537	-1864	0301	7575	0689	4353	1073	-3682	5641	0520	5212	2796	2506	1806	3695	-2937	5583	-0712	3930	3932	3559	4411
WC2			2721	-1651	0273	7112	2519	6229	2203	-3554	4103	0082	3706	1972	2000	0837	5061	-4967	5273	-0094	3650	3260	3419	4812
EPP2				4867	3051	5695	3068	3131	-0460	-1926	3884	3173	4391	7917	3650	6460	4502	1077	-1905	-1714	9330	4989	8165	-1707
EFP2					-0570	1721	-0896	1317	-2423	-3134	1093	6358	2794	1259	2587	2982	3736	-0495	-1411	-3245	1938	7202	3244	-4577
ECP2						3563		2269	0719	-1821	3399	3640	4089	6864	5688	6824	2542	2795	-2212	-3018	7585	5043	8345	-3443
SERV2							0768	2817	0553	-1821	5213	5180	5688	6864	3852	4972	2542	-0389	-2974	-2160	6838	4198	5873	2830
AIDP2								4124		2161	-1320	0230	-0126	0170	0520	1824	4952	-0389	-3299	0844	2160	2046	2865	0290
UNION									3739	-3821	-0631	-0606	2397	2388	3386	1736	4635	-6678	1531	2834	3279	2694	3080	2496
UNEM2										-0939	2872	-0631	1238	-1205	1331	-0601	3053	-4140	3661	-0178	-0712	2121	-0721	1946
CEN2											-4155	-2775	-4521	-2290	-4051	-2913	-3411	4064	-2614	-0367	-2302	-5352	-3250	1431
FELP2												2206	9605	4525	2848	3405	2065	-0666	2850	-0110	4489	4610	4504	-0196
FIRP2													4833	1464	1079	1812	4704	-1499	-0995	-1112	2243	4824	2547	-3078
NEED2														4479	2864	3573	3195	-1026	2274	-0416	4669	5514	4769	-1054
NLP2															5725	8504	2071	2071	-0755	-0554	9321	4717	8601	-1056
NLF2																7408	3148	-1216	0401	-0331	5328	7288	6285	0288
NLC2																	2184	1991	-1372	-0715	7858	6203	9126	-1394
COST2																		-5680	0524	0346	3984	5643	3859	1295
SOUTH																			-2782		1230	-1901	0989	-2829
WEST																				-4098	-0767	1339	-0473	3474
CENT																					-3801	-2574	-1595	2438
XPP2																						5534	9038	-0411
XFP2																							6681	-1105
XCP2																								-0733

found between employment in police (*EPP*) and felonies per 1000 population (*FELP*), employment in fire (*EFP*), and fires per 1000 population (*FIRP*), and between employment in the common functions (*ECP*) and felonies plus fires per 1000 population (*NEED*). Finally, in the nonpayroll cost equations, relatively high correlations are evident between nonpayroll costs per 1000 population in police, fire and the common functions (*NLP, NLF,* and *NLC* respectively) and their corresponding employment variables (*EPP, EFP,* and *ECP*).

This intercorrelation matrix also suggests possible difficulties in interpreting the coefficients of some variables due to multicollinearity. In the wage equation, a relatively large correlation exists between the union (*UNION*) and southern region (*SOUTH*) variables, suggesting difficulty might be encountered in assessing their relative significance. Similarly, in the employment equation, correlation between the income (*INC*) and wage variables (*WP, WF* and *WC*) could also be troublesome. Finally, in the nonpayroll cost equation, such intercorrelation is evident between the price (*COST*) and southern region (*SOUTH*) variables. As a result of these intercorrelations, some care will have to be taken in the interpretation of the statistical results presented later in the chapter.

In concluding this section on the distribution of the dependent and independent variables, it is informative to determine the extent and significance of regional variation in the dependent variables—wages, employment, nonpayroll costs and expenditures. Table 3-4 presents the regional distribution of the mean values of each of these variables. These data indicate that wages were generally highest in the west and lowest in the south; employment was generally highest in the east and lowest in the west; expenditures were usually highest in the west in 1966 and in the east in 1971, but lowest in the central region in both years; no such conclusions could be drawn in the case of nonpayroll costs.[k]

Finally, the extent of regional variation in each of these variables was investigated through an analysis of variance. The results indicated that there was a significant pattern (at the 5 percent level) of regional variation in every case. The least significant regional pattern was exhibited by nonpayroll costs, while the most significant one was that for wages. It should also be noted that, although the results were slightly better for 1966 than 1971, the significance of the regional effects did not differ markedly between the two years.

---

[k]Although the U.S. Census Bureau includes Baltimore and Washington in the southern region, questions might arise concerning the effect on the mean values of the variables resulting from their inclusion in the eastern region. However, when these cities were included in the eastern regions, few changes in the relative positions among regions occurred except in the case of police employment. In that case, police employment in the South become the lowest of any region. Further, when the equations in the remainder of this chapter were fitted with data including Baltimore and Washington in the eastern region, little change in the significance of the variables occurred. In fact, of all the equations fitted (wages, employment, and nonpayroll costs), only in the case of police employment was the significance of a variable affected. In this case, the south variable exerted a significantly negative influence on police employment levels.

Table 3-4

The Regional Distribution of Wages, Employment, Nonpayroll Costs, and Current Expenditure Means for Selected Common Municipal Functions: 1966 and 1971

	Average Wages		Employment per 1000 Population		Nonpayroll Cost per 1000 Population[a]		Current Expenditure per 1000 Population	
	1966	1971	1966	1971	1966	1971	1966	1971
Police								
East	$7,209	$9,920	3.05	3.84	$3,070	$12,990	$25,678	$52,180
Central	7,017	9,437	2.40	2.87	3,134	13,918	20,093	41,375
South	6,550	9,035	2.46	3.40	4,010	19,662	20,862	52,447
West	7,770	10,801	2.16	2.69	7,261	12,971	24,021	42,186
U.S.	7,103	9,723	2.50	3.15	4,170	14,859	22,222	46,313
Fire								
East	6,911	9,513	2.27	2.59	2,164	7,596	17,695	31,952
Central	7,136	9,945	1.58	1.63	1,791	6,392	12,996	22,522
South	6,287	9,129	1.58	1.84	2,653	5,960	12,762	22,494
West	8,730	12,154	1.62	1.73	4,394	6,900	18,394	27,862
U.S.	7,221	10,121	1.73	1.90	2,607	6,547	15,013	25,545
All Common								
East	6,399	9,596	11.05	12.53	23,680	51,691	94,769	172,616
Central	6,722	9,568	8.78	9.77	21,082	46,869	80,537	141,394
South	5,421	8,075	10.57	12.37	27,623	64,707	85,912	167,203
West	8,121	11,321	8.49	9.67	32,856	40,080	102,032	149,252
U.S.	6,642	9,589	9.60	10.91	25,484	50,582	89,106	155,367

[a]Nonpayroll cost figures were estimated by subtracting payrolls in each function from current expenditure.

Source: See Table 3-2.

Regression Results

Results of the Wage Equations

Tables 3-5, 3-6, and 3-7 present the results of the wage regressions for police, fire, and the common functions. As suggested by these data, the opportunity wage (*SERV*) was the most significant factor in explaining public employee wages for each function in both years. For all equations, this variable was significantly positive at the 0.001 level of confidence. The significance of this variable is consistent with the concept of wage rollout from the private sector

Table 3-5

Coefficients and Standard Errors of Variables in Wage Regressions for Police: 1966 and 1971

	1966		1971	
	Case I	Case II	Case I	Case II
SERV	1.1988[c]	1.2828[c]	1.0886[c]	1.0851[c]
	(0.2401)	(0.3515)	(0.2200)	(0.2137)
AIDP	9.5193	13.3806	6.9188	7.1574
	(11.0089)	(16.1393)	(11.8092)	(11.3783)
UNEM	−14.0191	6.3062	−65.4349	−64.3459
	(193.5471)	(205.8212)	(79.6512)	(77.6296)
INC	0.3350	0.3165	0.3799	0.3784[a]
	(0.2433)	(0.2533)	(0.1901)	(0.1865)
UNION	20.1222	28.2028	57.8429	58,9607[b]
	(17.8943)	(30.3930)	(23.1160)	(19.8942)
SOUTH	−92.2199	−7.8134	−53.2962	−845.4065
	(422.5931)	(498.8274)	(534.1990)	(828.3564)
WEST	−496.4950	−638.3056	169.4784	191.8155
	(484.8002)	(651.9834)	(507.9849)	(448.6447)
CENT	−153.5153	−185.8268	−546.8299	−527.2922
	(336.1577)	(354.8952)	(426.8023)	(373.1189)
EPP		−154.7816		118.8487
		(466.7413)		(94.7746)
CONST	−1024.6204	−1095.4629	−1556.5978	−1588.2465
R^2	0.7012	0.7024	0.7439	0.7569

[a]Denotes significance at 0.05 level.

[b]Denotes significance at 0.01 level.

[c]Denotes significance at 0.001 level.

Note: Figures in parentheses are standard errors.

into the public sector. This hypothesis contends that, whether through a competition effect or a demonstration effect, wage increases gained in the private sector will tend to be matched by gains in the public sector.

Because of the possibility that multicollinearity led to dominance of this variable in the wage equation, an alternative specification, which omitted the opportunity wage variable, was attempted. In each case, the income variable replaced the opportunity wage variable as the single most important one in the regression. The existence of multicollinearity between the opportunity wage and the income variable, then, can be assumed to be hiding the significance of the income variable. In any case, these results indicate that the most important single determinant of public-sector wages is the level of living of the community (no matter whether measured in terms of private sector earnings or personal income). However, it is not possible to determine whether this importance

Table 3-6
Coefficients and Standard Errors of Variables in Wage Regressions for Fire: 1966 and 1971

	1966		1971	
	Case I	Case II	Case I	Case II
SERV	1.0912[c]	1.0912[c]	1.4954[c]	1.4361[c]
	(0.2231)	(0.2271)	(0.2548)	(0.2611)
AIDP	5.9733	5.9190	0.8540	−0.8175
	(10.2330)	(11.4895)	(13.6753)	(13.7636)
UNEM	−100.9927	−101.3200	−165.3697	−198.7718[a]
	(179.9061)	(185.3171)	(92.2378)	(97.8111)
INC	0.4225	0.4230	0.1340	0.2605
	(0.2262)	(0.2337)	(0.2202)	(0.2526)
UNION	27.7258	27.7584	43.1303	54.6875
	(16.6332)	(17.1677)	(26.7689)	(29.048)
SOUTH	−15.7973	−13.0454	3.6050	478.1252
	(392.8091)	(469.5262)	(618.6138)	(773.5013)
WEST	789.5641	791.5667	2076.7759[b]	2449.6081[b]
	(450.6319)	(492.2262)	(588.2573)	(692.1009)
CENT	136.0304	138.0840	581.7905	970.4039
	(312.4657)	(367.2567)	(494.2462)	(623.6289)
EFP		4.3051		552.4948
		(385.8461)		(541.3195)
CONST	−1477.3259	−1490.5054	−571.0644	−3130.2374
R^2	0.8165	0.8165	0.7869	0.7944

[a]Denotes significance at 0.05 level.
[b]Denotes significance at 0.01 level.
[c]Denotes significance at 0.001 level.
Note: Figures in parentheses are standard errors.

results from a rollout of wages from the private to the public sector, to the existence of a fiscal capacity which is adequate to pay high wages, or both of these factors.

The other variables in the equations were generally insignificant. Exceptions to this are the west regional dummy (in four equations) and the union variable (in three equations). Due to the fact that the east region was omitted, the significant west dummy variable suggests that employees in this region have been successful in obtaining wages in excess of those of similar public employees in the east. Since the union variable measures private (rather than public) unionism, the results indicate that, either through a demonstration effect on public-sector wage demands, or through an encouraging effect on public-employee unions, areas with a high degree of unionization are associated with higher public-employee wages.

Table 3-7

Coefficients and Standard Errors of Variables in the Wage Regressions for Common Functions: 1966 and 1971

	1966		1971	
	Case I	Case II	Case I	Case II
SERV	0.8855[b]	0.7915[a]	1.1380[c]	1.1907[c]
	(0.2541)	(0.2955)	(0.1973)	(0.3162)
AIDP	0.0396	−5.8068	10.9178	11.3385
	(11.6516)	(14.2776)	(10.5914)	(10.9391)
UNEM	15.4039	101.0805	−125.8455	−135.0186
	(204.8470)	(238.3154)	(71.4371)	(84.1387)
INC	0.4133	0.4509	0.2525	0.2197
	(0.2576)	(0.2421)	(0.1705)	(0.2307)
UNION	21.8979	14.4284	55.8539[a]	58.9498[a]
	(18.9391)	(22.2472)	(20.7322)	(25.4944)
SOUTH	−523.8825	−609.4006	−742.6721	−686.7886
	(447.2653)	(436.5853)	(479.1090)	(551.5516)
WEST	675.6386	847.3084	1253.9602[b]	1202.8394[a]
	(513.1042)	(527.7604)	(455.5982)	(520.1515)
CENT	203.6919	295.8072	34.6797	−12.5244
	(355.7836)	(380.4563)	(382.7877)	(446.3546)
ECP		67.7861		−34.9048
		(131.5506)		(161.8288)
CONST	−1085.6674	−1663.1699	−641.6326	−263.0084
R^2	0.7642	0.7683	0.8431	0.8433

[a]Denotes significance at the 0.05 level.

[b]Denotes significance at the 0.01 level.

[c]Denotes significance at the 0.001 level.

Note: Figures in parentheses are standard errors.

The alternative specifications of the wage equation appear to have had little effect on the ability of the equation to explain public-sector wages. In no equation was the employment variable significant. Although the inclusion of the employment variable raised the coefficient of determination (as expected), it also lowered the F value of the regression and increased the standard error of the estimate. The fact that the employment variable was not significant in any equation should be emphasized. This result suggests that wage rates are determined without consideration of employment levels.

In terms of significant variables and goodness of fit, no large difference between the results obtained for equations in the two years was observed. However, two patterns were noteworthy. In the 1966 regressions, only the opportunity wage variable was significant, while in the 1971 regressions, other variables (*WEST* and *UNION*) were also important. Further, while the fit was slightly better for police and the common functions in 1971 than in 1966, the opposite was the case for fire.

Table 3-8 shows the beta coefficients—the beta coefficient or partial regression coefficient indicates the change in the dependent variable per unit change in the independent variable—and their ranks for the wage equations which exclude employment (case I). As expected by its high level of significance, the opportunity wage was the most important variable in each equation, followed generally by the west regional dummy and the income variable. It should also be noted that, while the opportunity wage was most important in every equation, its importance (relative to the second most important variable) decreased between 1966 and 1971. This could suggest a relative decline in the importance of local differences and the increase in the importance of regional factors.

Before proceeding with the results of the employment equation, mention should again be made of the existence of the problem of multicollinearity. Of particular note are the correlations that exist between the income and opportunity wage variables and the south and union variables, as well as between the union and income variables. It is highly possible that these intercorrelations have led to the dominance of the opportunity wage in these equations.

Table 3-8
Beta Coefficients and Their Ranks for Wage Regressions for Police, Fire, and Common Functions: 1966 and 1971

	Police		Fire		Common Functions	
	1966	1971	1966	1971	1966	1971
SERV	0.7106	0.5542	0.5454	0.5886	0.4406	0.4965
	(1)	(1)	(1)	(1)	(1)	(1)
AIDP	0.0963	0.0629	0.0509	0.0061	0.0003	0.0866
	(6)	(6)	(7)	(7)	(8)	(7)
UNEM	−0.0110	−0.0899	−0.0665	−0.1790	0.0101	−0.1510
	(8)	(5)	(5)	(4)	(7)	(5)
INC	0.2168	0.2288	0.2306	0.0635	0.2245	0.1327
	(3)	(3)	(3)	(6)	(2)	(6)
UNION	0.1694	0.3514	0.1969	0.2064	0.1548	0.2962
	(5)	(2)	(4)	(3)	(5)	(3)
SOUTH	−0.3696	−0.0154	−0.0053	0.0008	−0.1763	−0.1875
	(2)	(8)	(8)	(8)	(4)	(4)
WEST	−0.1907	0.0470	0.2558	0.4533	0.2179	0.3034
	(4)	(7)	(2)	(2)	(3)	(2)
CENT	−0.0701	−0.1801	0.0524	0.1509	0.0780	0.0100
	(7)	(4)	(6)	(5)	(6)	(8)

Note: Figures in parentheses are the ranks of the beta coefficients.

Results of the Employment Regressions

Tables 3-9, 3-10, and 3-11 show the results of the employment regressions for the three functions and two years being studied. For police and the common functions, the service needs measures (felonies and felonies plus fires per 1000 population respectively) were significant at the 5 percent level in two and three of the equations respectively. For fire, the service needs measure (fires per 1000 population) was significant at the .001 level.

It has been indicated previously that a significant relationship between service needs and employment levels can result from the operation of several forces. On the one hand, citizens recognizing increased crime rates or incidents of fire might pressure city hall to cause city officials (wishing to stay in office) to respond by raising employment levels. On the other, increasing workload might cause city employees to pressure their superiors into increasing employment to ease the burden of work on the average employee.

In the common functions as well as police equations, the wage variable was significantly negative in only one equation, while for fire, this variable was

Table 3-9
Coefficients and Standard Errors of Variables in the Employment Regressions for Police: 1966 and 1971

	1966		1971	
	Case I	Case II	Case I	Case II
FELP	0.0406[a]	0.0265[a]	0.0231[a]	0.0067
	(0.0149)	(0.0127)	(0.0102)	(0.0117)
AIDP	0.0261[a]	0.0208	0.0178	0.0114
	(0.0122)	(0.0113)	(0.0131)	(0.0115)
INC	−0.0003	−0.0005	−0.0002	−0.0007
	(0.0003)	(0.0003)	(0.0003)	(0.0004)
CEN	0.0076	0.0111	−0.0020	0.0055
	(0.0074)	(0.0069)	(0.0099)	(0.0089)
WP	−0.0001	−0.0002	−0.0004[a]	−0.0002
	(0.0001)	(0.002)	(0.0002)	(0.0002)
SOUTH	−0.4921	−0.3400	0.1660	0.4650
	(0.4241)	(0.3915)	(0.5658)	(0.4986)
WEST	−0.8009	−0.5933	−0.4717[a]	−1.0923
	(0.4963)	(0.4601)	(0.6261)	(0.5549)
CENT	−0.4353	−0.1872	−0.6345	0.0393
	(0.3841)	(0.3639)	(0.5370)	(0.5110)
CONST	1.6210	1.5010	0.0455	0.7599
R^2	0.5048	0.5878	0.5473	0.6610

[a]Denotes significance at 0.05 level.
Note: Figures in parentheses are standard errors.

Table 3-10

Coefficients and Standard Errors of the Variables in the Employment Regressions for Fire: 1966 and 1971

	1966		1971	
	Case I	Case II	Case I	Case II
FIRP	0.0528[c]	0.0527[c]	0.0558[c]	0.0587[c]
	(0.0134)	(0.0135)	(0.0149)	(0.0147)
AIDP	0.0130[a]	0.0131[a]	0.0060	0.0067
	(0.0060)	(0.0062)	(0.0057)	(0.0056)
INC	0.0002	0.0002	−0.00001	0.00001
	(0.0002)	(0.0002)	(0.0001)	(0.0001)
CEN	−0.0085[a]	−0.0086[a]	−0.0080	−0.0095[a]
	(0.0038)	(0.0041)	(0.0042)	(0.0042)
WF	−0.0001	−0.0001[a]	−0.0001	−0.0002[a]
	(0.0001)	(0.0001)	(0.0001)	(0.0001)
SOUTH	−0.2353	−0.2352	−0.2172	−0.1861
	(0.2071)	(0.2093)	(0.2458)	(0.2410)
WEST	−0.4031	−0.3986	−0.3088	−0.2148
	(0.2465)	(0.2544)	(0.2771)	(0.2804)
CENT	−0.5060[b]	−0.5073[a]	−0.5684[a]	−0.5620[a]
	(0.1838)	(0.1864)	(0.2133)	(0.2081)
CONST	0.7754	0.7721	2.6307	2.6400
R^2	0.6233	0.6153	0.6521	0.6691

[a]Denotes significance at the 0.05 level.

[b]Denotes significance at the 0.01 level.

[c]Denotes significance at the 0.001 level.

Note: Figures in parentheses are standard errors.

significant in two equations. As hypothesized above, a negative coefficient for the wage variable can result from the existence of some sort of budget constraint whereby a particular city, at the margin, can obtain increased employment levels only by paying lower wages. Given what is generally known about the public sector, it is likely that these results indicate the operation of a budget constraint.

For three of the four fire regressions, the centralization variable was also significantly negative. However, the significance of this variable for only fire (not police or the common functions) is somewhat more difficult to interpret. Apparently the size of the nonresidential population only places demands on the city's fire protection. This might arise out of a need to protect from fire the buildings in which suburban employees work. It is interesting to note however, that a similar need is not apparent in the case of police. Clearly more research is needed to fully explain the reasons for this result.

Regional differences were also observed in both the fire and common function equations. For fire, employment in the central region was significantly

38

Table 3-11

Coefficients and Standard Errors of Variables in the Employment Regressions for the Common Functions: 1966 and 1971

	1966		1971	
	Case I	Case II	Case I	Case II
NEED	0.0719[a]	0.0410	0.0614[a]	0.0461[a]
	(0.0295)	(0.0332)	(0.0238)	(0.0206)
AIDP	0.0542	0.0496	0.0485	0.0369
	(0.0289)	(0.0277)	(0.0304)	(0.0293)
INC	−0.0005	−0.0014	−0.0001	−0.0006
	(0.0007)	(0.0008)	(0.0006)	(0.0006)
CEN	−0.0061	0.0029	−0.0203	−0.0144
	(0.0177)	(0.0176)	(0.0223)	(0.0213)
WC	−0.0005	−0.0005	−0.0003[a]	−0.0003
	(0.0004)	(0.0007)	(0.0002)	(0.0003)
SOUTH	0.6159	1.3499	1.5197	2.1504
	(1.0191)	(1.0573)	(1.2998)	(1.2649)
WEST	−2.6505[a]	−3.2682[a]	−3.3965[a]	−3.7554[b]
	(1.2061)	(1.2018)	(1.3840)	(1.3218)
CENT	−1.7267	−1.5316	−2.3216[a]	−1.9596
	(0.8982)	(0.8627)	(1.1192)	(1.0734)
CONST	8.2520	9.5070	6.2784	6.6566
R^2	0.5326	0.5759	0.5430	0.5895

[a]Denotes significance at the 0.05 level.

[b]Denotes significance at the 0.01 level.

Note: Figures in parentheses are standard errors.

below that of the east (the standard for comparison), while for the common functions, employment in the west was significantly below the east.

The alternative formulation of the wage equation (specified to include employment) generally had little effect on the employment equations. For both fire and the common functions, the alternative specification did not affect the sign of any coefficients nor their significance and changed their magnitude only slightly. However, for police in 1966, both service and need and aid were significant only under the simple wage formulation (excluding employment), while for 1971, a similar situation occurred when needs and the west regional dummy were both significant only in the simple formulation. The fact that the alternate specification had little effect on the employment equation is hardly surprising, however, since it had relatively little effect on the wage equation.

The beta coefficients and their ranks shown in Table 3-12 help shed some light on the relative importance of the variables for the simple formulation of the model (excluding employment in the wage equation). These coefficients indicate the relative importance of the service need and west variables for all functions in both years.

Table 3-12
Beta Coefficients and Their Ranks for Employment Regressions for Police, Fire, and Common Functions: 1966 and 1971

	Police		Fire		Common Functions	
	1966	1971	1966	1971	1966	1971
NEED	0.4229	0.3052	0.5067	0.4789	0.3504	0.3959
	(1)	(3)	(1)	(1)	(3)	(2)
AIDP	0.3099	0.1892	0.2691	0.1307	0.2573	0.2254
	(3)	(5)	(5)	(7)	(4)	(4)
INC	−0.1962	−0.1259	0.2369	−0.0167	−0.1578	−0.0340
	(7)	(6)	(6)	(8)	(6)	(8)
CEN	0.1649	−0.0326	−0.3224	−0.2709	−0.0533	−0.1468
	(8)	(8)	(3)	(4)	(8)	(7)
WAGE	−0.2423	−0.4668	−0.2345	−0.2746	−0.2531	−0.1499
	(4)	(2)	(7)	(3)	(5)	(6)
SOUTH	−0.2312	0.0561	−0.1931	−0.1500	0.1159	0.2248
	(6)	(7)	(8)	(6)	(7)	(5)
WEST	−0.3610	−0.4770	−0.3170	−0.2044	−0.4779	−0.4815
	(2)	(1)	(4)	(5)	(1)	(1)
CENT	−0.2329	−0.2443	−0.4727	−0.4470	−0.3699	−0.3910
	(5)	(4)	(2)	(2)	(2)	(3)

Note: Figures in parentheses are the ranks of the beta coefficients.

Results of the Nonpayroll Cost Regressions

Table 3-13 presents the results of the nonpayroll cost regressions for police, fire and the common functions. As indicated there, the employment variable was significant and positive in four of the six equations. The significance of the employment variable suggests that nonpayroll costs are related to employment. As suggested above, this could be the result of the existence of a production function of fixed proportions, whereby employment levels determine the nonpayroll items to be purchased.

In addition to the wage variable, the west regional dummy was significantly positive in four of the six regions, while the central dummy was significantly positive in two of the six equations. These results are particularly interesting when compared with those of the previous section which indicated that the coefficient for these two regions in the employment equations for several functions were significantly negative. Given the fact that nonpayroll costs include expenditures on contractual services, as well as some capital expenditures (among other items), it is entirely possible that cities in these regions are able to maintain service levels with fewer employees directly on the payroll. However, the determination of the magnitude of this contracting out of services is well beyond the scope of this study.

It is also possible to interpret these figures as indication of a greater nonlabor

Table 3-13

Coefficients and Standard Errors of Variables in Nonpayroll Equations for Police, Fire, and the Common Functions: 1966 and 1971

	Police		Fire		Common Functions	
	1966	1971	1966	1971	1966	1971
EMP	1270.69[a]	9179.62[c]	2673.03[b]	1555.39	1052.13	9506.67[c]
	(519.29)	(1207.77)	(836.79)	(1390.19)	(905.55)	(2043.29)
COST	−1.2227	−0.8236	2.2147[a]	1.8370	2.8551	10.9386
	(1.2564)	(2.6030)	(1.0361)	(1.2596)	(5.1047)	(9.4565)
SOUTH	492.15	9548.91	189.15	1939.46	7257.16	30,698.59
	(1698.54)	(5006.37)	(1461.22)	(2781.84)	(7061.21)	(19,732.93)
WEST	5221.91[c]	10,083.59[a]	3802.02[b]	1826.23	11,837.27[a]	22,564.64
	(1348.69)	(3897.21)	(1204.42)	(2443.84)	(5684.26)	(15,840.84)
CENT	542.83	9328.09[a]	853.57	1542.59	606.49	28,939.74[a]
	(1198.04)	(3530.06)	(1115.67)	(2321.67)	(5086.93)	(14,414.37)
CONST	10,878.99	−12,710.75	17,255.29	−17,818.45	−15,232.31	−19,478.40
R^2	0.3950	0.7249	0.3727	0.1393	0.2168	0.5290

[a]Denotes significance at the 0.05 level.

[b]Denotes significance at the 0.01 level.

[c]Denotes significance at the 0.001 level.

Note: Figures in parentheses are standard errors.

intensity in the production process in these two regions. Because of the existence of different production functions, cities in these regions might employ less labor and more nonlabor inputs relative to the amounts employed in the east (the regional standard). It should be noted, however, that the relative merits of these explanations, given the aggregative nature of the nonpayroll cost data, are difficult to assess. Such a determination would require the gathering of highly detailed data from a number of cities, and is well beyond the scope of this study.

The fit of most of these nonpayroll cost equations (also indicated in Table 3-13) was much poorer and indicated more variation than those obtained for the wage and employment equations. A substantial amount of this is certainly due to data incomparabilities resulting from different treatment of nonlabor inputs in the accounting of total expenditure among cities and also between 1966 and 1971. As already noted, some nonpayroll costs might be considered capital expenditure and excluded from current expenditure. Further, nonpayroll costs include pension and fringe benefit costs as well as the cost of materials and supplies.

The beta coefficients shown in Table 3-14 allow a comparison of the relative importance of the variables. Ranked in terms of these coefficients, the employment and west variables were the two most important ones in most equations. However, it should be noted that the relative importance of the employment

Table 3-14
Beta Coefficients and Their Ranks for Nonpayroll Cost Regression for Police, Fire, and Common Functions: 1966 and 1971

	Police		Fire		Common Functions	
	1966	1971	1966	1971	1966	1971
EMP	0.3774 (2)	0.9005 (1)	0.5446 (2)	0.2303 (2)	0.2164 (3)	0.6968 (1)
COST	−0.2049 (3)	−0.0474 (5)	0.4462 (3)	0.3259 (1)	0.1326 (4)	0.2057 (5)
SOUTH	0.0687 (5)	0.3168 (4)	0.0317 (5)	0.1984 (3)	0.2808 (2)	0.3329 (3)
WEST	0.6985 (1)	0.3206 (3)	0.6115 (1)	0.1791 (5)	0.4390 (1)	0.2345 (4)
CENT	0.0863 (4)	0.3523 (2)	0.1631 (4)	0.1796 (4)	0.0267 (5)	0.3573 (2)

Note: Figures in parentheses are ranks of the beta coefficients.

variable increased (or stayed the same) while that of the west variable decreased between 1966 and 1971. This might suggest the dwindling of regional differences and the increased importance of local demands in the determination of the level of nonpayroll costs.

Synthesis of the Results

The Relationship between Estimated and Observed Expenditures

In order to determine the extent of the ability of the model to explain expenditure variation, observed values of expenditures per 1000 population were regressed upon estimated values of the expenditures (that is, estimated nonpayroll costs plus the product of estimated wages and employment levels). The results of these simple regressions (shown in Table 3-15) indicate that significant (at the 0.001 level of confidence) amounts of variation in actual expenditures can be explained by the estimates of expenditures obtained from this model. Best fits were obtained for regressions involving police and the common functions in 1971 (explaining about 88 percent and 81 percent of the variation respectively), while poorer fits were obtained for the fire regressions in both years. The increased explanatory power of the police and common function models between 1966 and 1971 is primarily the result of variation in nonlabor cost estimates (see Table 3-13), and defies explanation due to the aggregative nature of the data.

Table 3-15

Coefficients and Standard Errors of the Variables in the Expenditure Regressions for Police, Fire, and Common Functions: 1966 and 1971

	Estimated Expenditure	Constant	R^2
Police			
1966	1.0859c (0.1236)	−1662.50	0.6758
1971	1.2351c (0.0759)	−8031.56	0.8774
Fire			
1966	1.1137c (0.1561)	−5398.38	0.5790
1971	1.0785c (0.1613)	−1185.40	0.5470
Common Functions			
1966	1.1258c (0.1439)	−9186.52	0.6230
1971	(1.4816c (0.1171)	−30,708.60	0.8123

cDenotes significance at the 0.001 level.
Note: Figures in parentheses are standard errors.

In order to better assess the explanatory power of the model, the regional distribution of estimated and observed expenditures is shown in Table 3-16. In general the results indicate that best estimates were obtained for eastern cities while poorest estimates were obtained for the south and west. Specifically, poorest estimates for police were registered in the south, while poorest in the common functions were those of the west. Poorest estimates of fire expenditures were for the south in 1966 and the west in 1971.

These differences in the explanatory power of the model across regions raises questions concerning the existence of a statistically significant regional pattern of variation in the ratios of estimated to observed expenditures. When the analysis of variance technique was employed, it was found that a distinct regional pattern of variation in these ratios existed. Stated differently, there was a significantly smaller variation in these ratios within each region (east, central, west, and south) than existed among these regions.

The implications of this result suggest the importance of considering these regional characteristics in any cross-section analysis of expenditures across regions. Further, this finding is particularly noteworthy in light of the fact that

Table 3-16

The Regional Distribution of the Means of Estimated and Observed Expenditures for Selected Functions: 1966 and 1971 (Amounts per 1000 Population)

	Police		Fire		All Common Functions	
	1966	1971	1966	1971	1966	1971
East						
Estimated	$25,467	$50,046	$20,627	$31,296	$93,437	$177,706
Observed	25,678	52,180	17,695	31,952	94,769	172,616
Estimated/Observed	0.992	0.959	1.166	0.979	0.986	1.029
Central						
Estimated	$19,913	$39,403	$16,290	$21,782	$78,702	$145,617
Observed	20,093	41,375	12,996	22,522	80,537	141,394
Estimated/Observed	0.991	0.952	1.253	0.967	0.977	1.030
South						
Estimated	$20,356	$49,624	$16,287	$21,978	$84,396	$169,851
Observed	20,862	52,446	12,762	22,494	85,912	167,202
Estimated/Observed	0.976	0.946	1.276	0.977	0.982	1.016
West						
Estimated	$24,009	$39,675	$21,887	$26,695	$ 99,516	$156,304
Observed	24,021	42,186	18,394	27,862	102,032	149,252
Estimated/Observed	0.999	0.940	1.190	0.958	0.975	1.047
United States						
Estimated	$21,995	$44,001	$18,327	$24,786	$87,308	$159,984
Observed	22,222	46,313	15,013	25,545	89,108	155,367
Estimated/Observed	0.990	0.950	1.221	0.970	0.980	1.030

the functions studied here are supposedly common to all municipalities across the nation. Some explanation of the existence of this pattern, as outlined previously, relate to the possibility of variation in functional responsibility as well as attitudes of the citizens toward the public sector. However, considerably more study than possible here is required to fully explain those factors underlying this regional variation.

Implications Concerning the Expenditure
Determination 'Process'

The results of the regression analysis indicate that one variable in each of the estimated equations was consistently significant, regardless of the function or year considered. In the wage equation, this important variable was identified as being the opportunity wage. Its significance suggests the importance of the wage rollout process in explaining public-sector wage rates. It was argued that this result can obtain from the operation of two forces. First, competition between public and private sectors for similar employees can cause wage increases in the private sector to place upward pressure on public-sector wages. Secondly, a demonstration effect between labor unions in the sectors could cause public employee unions to demand similar wage increases to those obtained by private-sector unions.

In the employment equation, the factor which proved to be a consistently good explainer was the service needs variable. The significance of this variable implies the importance of a relationship between perceived service needs and employment levels. The process through which this relationship operates involves two forces. First, citizens might pressure city officials to increase employment as a result of the deterioration in the quality of the service caused by the increased workload of city employees. Secondly, city employees might pressure city officials to add employees because of an increase in the amount of work they are asked to perform.

In the nonpayroll cost equation, employment was consistently significant. This significance implies the possible existence of a fixed proportions production function. The existence of such a production function would result in a demand for nonlabor quantities roughly proportionate to the level of employment. Given the typical labor intensity characterizing the production of many (if not most) government services, this explanation appears highly plausible.

4

The Historical Growth in New York City Governmental Expenditures

In the previous chapter, a model of the expenditure determination process was applied to explain cross-sectional variation in expenditure *levels* for a sample of thirty-nine U.S. cities. However, while cross-sectional analysis is useful to some in identifying the factors underlying expenditure variation among cities, it is the time-series analysis of expenditures for particular cities, with its emphasis on explaining expenditure *growth*, which is of most relevance to the local officials. The specific purpose here, therefore, is to demonstrate the usefulness of this model in explaining historical growth in expenditures for a particular city as well as demonstrate how the model might be used to predict future expenditure growth.

Accordingly, the remainder of this chapter is divided into four sections. In the second section the focus is on an analysis of the structure and percentage growth in wages, employment, and nonpayroll costs for six large New York City departments over the 1965 to 1972 period. The third section provides a breakdown of payroll and nonpayroll cost growth into their component parts. In the fourth section the growth in wages, employment, and nonpayroll costs is compared with that of factors suggested by the cross-sectional model. The final section demonstrates the forecasting abilities of the model and suggests areas for future research.

Empirical Specification of the Time-Series Model

Recalling the model in Chapter 2 and applying it to time-series analysis, the following equations apply:

$$\hat{W}^i = f(W_O, F, U, M, \hat{E}_p^i, T) \tag{4.1}$$

$$\hat{E}_p^i = f(S_p^i, C, F, \hat{W}^i, T) \tag{4.2}$$

$$N\hat{C}_p^i = f(\hat{E}_p^i, P, T) \tag{4.3}$$

where:

W_O = opportunity wage of public employer

F = fiscal capacity of citizens

U = extent of unionization

M = mobility

S_p^i = service need of citizens per 1000 population in function i

C = centralization of population with the SMSA

P = market determined price of nonlabor inputs

T = temporal influences

Before proceeding, however, it is helpful to point out that the following analysis differs in two respects from that of the previous chapter. First, the estimation technique employed here is nonstochastic in nature, and divides growth in the aggregate variables payroll costs and nonpayroll costs into amounts attributable to growth in each of its component variables, that is, real wages, employment, and prices. In other words, the equations which will be analyzed in the third section are of the following form:

$$\Delta LC^i = f(\Delta W^{\prime i}, \Delta P^i, \Delta E^i) \tag{4.4}$$

$$\Delta NC^i = f(\Delta P^i, \Delta E^i) \tag{4.5}$$

where:

LC^i = payroll costs in function i

NC^i = nonpayroll costs in function i

$W^{\prime i}$ = real wage rates in function i

P^i = consumer price level in function i

E^i = employment level in function i

Δ = change in a variable over time

This technique was used because of the difficulty in obtaining sufficiently detailed time-series data necessary for regression analysis. It should be recognized also that the effect of inflation on wage rates as well as nonpayroll expenditures is explicitly taken into account in this analysis. This variable was omitted from an analysis of wage rates in the previous chapter because of its high correlation with the other determinants of public employee wages.

Second, because of the difficulty in obtaining the time-series data mentioned above, the explanation of growth in the dependent variables (W^i, E^i and NC^i) will involve only a comparison of their growth with that of the variables identified by cross-sectional analysis to be the most important determinants (W_o, S, E^i). The equation to be analyzed in the fourth section, then, is of the following form:

$$\Delta W^i = f(\Delta W_o) \qquad (4.1A)$$

$$\Delta E^i = f(\Delta S^i) \qquad (4.2A)$$

$$\Delta NC^i = f(\Delta E^i) \qquad (4.3A)$$

where:

W^i = money wage rates in function i

S^i = service needs of citizens in function i

The departments which will be studied in the above context include police, fire, environmental protection (EPA), social services, education and higher education for the years 1965 and 1972.[a] Since EPA was not in existence in 1965, it was necessary to estimate relevant labor cost and nonlabor cost data by aggregating the 1965 figures for the departments which eventually were combined to form the Environmental Protection Administration.

The labor cost data for each department was compiled according to each of five job classifications: executive, uniformed or delivery, laborer, clerical, and other. Executives include the highest paid administrative personnel. Uniformed or delivery personnel include those who actually perform the service to the public (for example, policemen, firemen, teachers, and so forth). The laborer category includes both skilled and unskilled maintenance employees. Clerical is made up of secretaries, filists, messengers, and other similar office workers. The other category, then, includes basically skilled professional and technical personnel not included in the previous categories.[b]

The data used for this analysis were obtained from the *New York City Executive Budgets* for the fiscal years 1965 and 1972 and therefore may periodically vary from actual employment figures due to job vacancies. The bias for employment figures, then, is almost certainly on the high side. However,

[a]Expenditures by these six departments accounted for 61 percent of New York City total current expenditure in 1965 and 65.5 percent of total current expenditure in 1972.

[b]Appendix C provides a more complete listing of the occupations in each category.

given the desire to disaggregate employment in the manner described, budget figures represent the only data source.

The Interdepartmental Structure and Growth
in New York City Expenditures

As indicated in Table 4-1, employment in these six departments increased between 1965 and 1972 from about 140,000 to about 200,000 (41.3 percent). In terms of departmental differences, growth in employment was faster in the education, higher education, and social services than in police, fire, or environmental protection. It should also be noted that growth in employment of uniformed-delivery personnel was among the slowest of any job category in each department, as well as the slowest of any category for the six departments combined.

Wage rates for the departments and job categories combined (as shown in Table 4-2) averaged $8,074 in 1965 and $12,888 in 1972, an increase of 59.6 percent. In contrast to the growth of employment, wages grew faster for police, fire, and environmental protection than for education, higher education or social services. Further, wage rates of uniformed-delivery personnel grew more rapidly than those of most job categories in each department and faster than those of any job category for the six departments combined.

The breakdown of expenditures into payroll and nonpayroll costs for each of the six departments is shown in Table 4-3. For the departments combined, nontransfer expenditures increased from about $1.7 billion to $3.9 billion between 1965 and 1972. Worthy of note is the fact that the importance of nonpayroll costs varied widely among departments, ranging from about 14 percent in social services (excluding transfer payments) to about 36 percent for education. It should also be noted that nonpayroll expenditures increased more rapidly than payroll expenditures in environmental protection, higher education, and social services (excluding transfers), while the reverse was true for the remaining departments. Finally, the departments with the fastest rates of growth in nonpayroll costs (environmental protection, higher education, and social services) also registered the greatest total expenditure increases.

In conclusion, these data suggest several important findings. First, wages grew faster and employment slower for workers in police, fire, and environmental protection than for those in education, higher education, or social services. Secondly, wages grew faster and employment slower for uniformed-delivery personnel than for nonuniformed-nondelivery workers. Third, nonpayroll expenditures grew faster than payroll expenditures for environmental protection, higher education, and social services, than for the remaining departments. Fourth, the three departments exhibiting the fastest growth in nonpayroll expenditure also registered the fastest rate of increase in current expenditure.

The Components of Growth in New York City Government Expenditures[c,d]

Payroll Costs

Having compared rates of growth for payroll and nonpayroll costs, it would be useful at this point to analyze that growth in terms of the growth in the components of these costs. Specifically, it would be helpful to be able to divide growth in payroll costs into amounts due to employment, price level, and real wage growth; and nonpayroll cost growth into that due to price level growth and real quantity growth.

The procedure used in this regard is quite simple. For payroll costs, the aim is to obtain an equation of the form

$$\Delta LC = l_1 \Delta E + l_2 \Delta P + l_3 \Delta W' \tag{4.6}$$

where:

LC = payroll costs

E = employment

P = price level

W' = real wages

This can be obtained by differentiating the following

$$dEPW' = \lim_{\Delta \to 0} (E + \Delta E)(W' + \Delta W')(P + \Delta P) - EW'P \tag{4.7}$$

$$= EW'\Delta P + EP\Delta W' + W'P\Delta E + E\Delta W'\Delta P$$

$$+ W'\Delta E\Delta P + P\Delta W'\Delta E + \Delta E\Delta W'\Delta P$$

To put (4.7) in the form called for in (4.6), all that is necessary is to allocate all the terms involving two or more deltas (Δ) among those with only one delta (Δ). In what follows, each of the three terms (hereafter referred to as the price, real wage, and employment components) is expressed as a percentage of the total change in payroll costs for the department or job category in question.[e] The

---

[c]For a detailed discussion of the methodology employed in this section, see Appendix D.

[d]For a similar application of the methodology used in this section, see Greytak, Gustely and Dinkelmeyer (28).

[e]These percentage components should not be confused with the percentage rates of growth in each of the individual variables. While percentage growth rates indicate the magnitude of increases in a particular variable over its initial value, these components indicate the percentage (or fraction) of the growth in the aggregate variable which can be attributed to growth in each component. It is therefore possible that the employment components for two departments could be very different even though employment in each department grew identically.

Table 4-1
Employment Levels by Department and Job Category: 1965 and 1972

Department Job Category	1965		1972		Percentage Change 1965-72
	Number Employees	Percentage of Departmental Total	Number Employees	Percentage of Departmental Total	
Police					
Executive	8	–	13	–	62.5
Uniformed	26,734	95.3	31,895	92.0	19.3
Laborer	871	3.1	1,334	3.8	53.2
Clerical	348	1.2	691	2.0	98.6
Other	102	0.4	752	2.2	637.3
Departmental Total	28,063	(19.9)	34,685	(17.4)	23.6
Fire					
Executive	4	–	6	–	50.0
Uniformed	13,199	94.3	13,592	92.5	2.3
Laborer	280	2.0	346	2.4	23.6
Clerical	224	1.6	262	1.8	17.0
Other	289	2.1	494	3.4	70.9
Departmental Total	13,996	(9.9)	14,700	(7.4)	5.0

Environmental Protection

Executive	25	0.1	52	0.3	108.0
Uniformed	11,405	60.6	12,124	58.9	6.3
Laborer	5,525	29.4	5,629	27.3	1.9
Clerical	837	4.4	1,253	6.1	49.7
Other	1,026	5.5	1,534	7.4	49.5
Departmental Total	18,818	(13.3)	20,592	(10.3)	9.4

Social Services

Executive	26	0.2	50	0.2	92.3
Delivery-Supervisor	1,594	11.2	3,165	10.2	98.6
Delivery-Investigator	5,240	36.1	7,544	24.2	44.0
Laborer	484	3.3	1,368	4.4	182.6
Clerical	4,904	33.8	13,559	43.5	176.5
Other	2,276	15.7	5,486	17.6	141.0
Departmental Total	14,524	(10.3)	31,172	(15.6)	114.6

Public Schools

Executive	100	0.1	271	0.3	171.0
Delivery-Principal	2,190	3.7	3,973	4.9	81.4
Delivery-Teacher	49,182	83.0	63,503	78.2	29.1
Laborer	1,708	2.9	2,069	3.2	50.4
Clerical	2,654	4.5	5,713	7.0	115.3
Other	3,398	5.7	5,168	6.4	52.1
Departmental Total	59,232	(42.0)	81,197	(40.7)	37.1

Table 4-1 (cont.)

Department Job Category	1965 Number Employees	1965 Percentage of Departmental Total	1972 Number Employees	1972 Percentage of Departmental Total	Percentage Change 1965-72
Higher Education					
Executive	42	0.6	115	0.7	173.8
Delivery-Professor	641	9.8	1,701	9.9	165.4
Delivery-Associate Professor	791	12.1	1,824	10.7	130.6
Delivery-Assistant Professor	1,239	18.9	3,075	18.0	148.2
Delivery-Instructor	1,059	16.1	2,919	17.1	175.6
Laborer	1,062	16.2	2,036	11.9	91.7
Clerical	953	14.5	3,006	17.6	215.4
Other	773	11.8	2,444	14.3	216.2
Departmental Total	6,650	(100.0)	17,120	(8.6)	161.0
Six Departments Combined		(4.6)			
Executive	205	0.1	507	0.3	147.3
Uniformed-Delivery	113,274	80.2	145,405	72.9	28.4
Laborer	9,930	7.0	13,282	6.7	33.8
Clerical	9,920	7.0	24,484	12.3	146.8
Other	7,864	5.6	15,788	7.9	100.8
Six Department Total	141,193	(100.0)	199,466	(100.0)	41.3

Source: *New York City Executive Budget and Supporting Schedules*, 1965-66 and 1972-73, (New York: Office of the Mayor, March 1965; March 1972).

Table 4-2
Average Wage Rates by Department and Job Category: 1965 and 1972

Department Job Category	1965		1972		Percentage Change 1965-72
	Salary	Percentage of Departmental Total	Salary	Percentage of Departmental Total	
Police					
Executive	$19,563	228.7	$28,670	205.1	46.6
Uniformed	8,685	101.5	14,489	103.6	66.8
Laborer	5,739	67.1	8,663	62.0	50.9
Clerical	4,918	57.5	6,572	47.0	33.6
Other	7,298	85.3	8,329	59.6	14.1
Departmental Average	8,554	(105.9)	13,979	(103.4)	63.4
Fire					
Executive	17,625	207.2	29,879	192.5	69.5
Uniformed	8,603	101.1	15,966	102.9	85.6
Laborer	8,385	98.6	12,460	80.3	48.3
Clerical	4,724	55.5	6,715	43.3	42.1
Other	7,051	82.9	9,981	64.3	41.6
Departmental Average	8,507	(105.3)	15,523	(120.4)	82.5
Environmental Protection					
Executive	15,536	212.0	25,854	208.6	66.4
Uniformed	7,421	101.2	12,678	102.3	70.8
Laborer	7,329	100.0	12,494	100.8	70.5
Clerical	4,945	67.5	7,575	61.1	53.2
Other	8,067	110.1	13,268	107.1	64.5
Departmental Average	7,330	(90.7)	12,394	(96.1)	69.1

Table 4-2 (cont.)

Department Job Category	1965		1972		Percentage Change 1965-72
	Salary	Percentage of Departmental Total	Salary	Percentage of Departmental Total	
Social Services					
Executive	15,148	261.4	24,710	266.4	63.1
Delivery-Supervisor	7,819	134.9	14,539	156.8	85.9
Delivery-Investigator	6,314	108.9	10,857	117.1	72.9
Laborer	5,178	89.3	7,655	82.5	47.8
Clerical	4,712	81.3	6,995	75.4	48.5
Other	5,546	95.7	9,960	107.4	79.6
Departmental Average	5,796	(71.7)	9,275	(71.9)	60.9
Public Schools					
Executive	21,291	249.3	27,974	217.8	31.4
Delivery-Principal	13,721	160.7	22,661	172.5	65.2
Delivery-Teacher	8,444	98.9	13,270	101.0	57.2
Laborer	7,557	88.5	10,163	79.1	34.5
Clerical	5,412	63.4	7,553	58.8	39.6
Other	7,581	88.8	11,026	85.8	45.4
Departmental Average	8,540	(105.7)	13,135	(101.9)	50.4

Higher Education

Executive	24,465	275.8	33,922	235.4	38.7
Delivery-Professor	17,119	193.0	26,638	184.9	55.6
Delivery-Associate Professor	12,617	142.2	20,579	142.8	63.1
Delivery-Assistant Professor	9,843	111.0	16,300	113.1	65.6
Delivery-Instructor	7,930	89.4	12,922	89.7	63.0
Laborer	5,179	58.4	8,159	56.6	57.5
Clerical	4,576	51.6	7,499	52.0	63.9
Other	7,460	84.1	13,475	93.5	80.6
Departmental Average	8,870	(100.0)	14,409	(111.8)	62.4

Six Departments Combined

Executive	20,333	251.8	28,824	223.6	41.7
Uniformed-Delivery	8,503	105.3	14,196	110.1	66.9
Laborer	6,924	85.7	10,495	81.4	51.5
Clerical	4,914	60.8	7,202	55.8	46.5
Other	7,020	86.9	11,154	86.5	58.8
Six Department Average	8,074	(100.0)	12,888	(100.0)	59.6

Source: *New York City Executive Budget and Supporting Schedules*, 1965-66 and 1972-73 (New York: Office of the Mayor, March 1965; March 1972).

Table 4-3
The Structure and Growth in Expenditures by Object for Six New York City Departments: 1965-1972 (Millions of Dollars)

	1965		1972		Percentage Growth
	Amount	Percentage of Department	Amount	Percentage of Department	
Police					
Payroll Cost	$238.2	72.2%	$485.8	74.5%	104.0%
Nonpayroll Cost	91.7	27.8	166.5	25.5	81.6
Current Expenditures	329.9	100.0	652.3	100.0	97.7
Fire					
Payroll Cost	121.7	71.9	223.2	74.3	83.4
Nonpayroll Cost	47.6	28.1	77.3	25.7	62.4
Current Expenditures	169.3	100.0	300.5	100.0	77.5
Environmental Protection					
Payroll Cost	120.6	86.4	250.1	81.6	107.4
Nonpayroll Cost	19.0	13.6	56.6	18.4	197.9
Current Expenditures	139.6	100.0	306.7	100.0	119.7
Public Schools					
Payroll Cost	572.8	64.0	1,413.2	72.8	146.7
Nonpayroll Cost	322.8	36.0	527.3	27.2	63.4
Current Expenditures	895.6	100.0	1,940.5	100.0	116.7

Higher Education					
Payroll Cost	75.4	85.1	288.2	75.4	282.2
Nonpayroll Cost	13.2	14.9	94.1	24.6	612.9
Current Expenditures	88.6 (419.6)	100.0	382.3	100.0	331.5
Social Service					
Payroll Cost	79.1	88.5	238.1	83.1	201.0
Nonpayroll Cost	10.3	11.5	48.5	16.9	370.9
Current Expenditures (Including Transfers)	89.4	100.0	286.6 (1,992.4)	100.0	220.6 (374.8)
Six Departments Combined					
Payroll Cost	1,207.8	70.5	2,898.6	74.9	140.0
Nonpayroll Cost	504.6	29.5	970.4	25.1	92.3
Current Expenditures (Including Transfers)	1,712.4 (2,042.6)	100.0	3,868.9 (5,574.7)	100.0	125.9 (172.9)

Source: *New York City Executive Budget and Supporting Schedules, 1965-66 and 1972-73* (New York: Office of the Mayor, March 1965; March 1972).

employment and wage data used to derive these estimates is that which was discussed above. The price level was estimated by use of the consumer price index for New York and northeastern New Jersey published by the Bureau of Labor Statistics.[f]

Each of the these components is shown for the six departments and five job categories in Table 4-4. For the departments and job categories combined, 43.8 percent of the increase in payroll costs can be attributed to employment increases (that is, the employment component), 43.7 percent to price increases (that is, the price component) and 12.7 percent to real wage increases (that is, the real wage component). The employment component ranged from a low of 5.9 percent in fire to a high of 74.8 percent in higher education. The price component ranged from 19.4 percent in higher education to 59.2 percent in EPA. The real wage component varied from a low in higher education of 5.8 percent to a high of 38.9 percent in the fire department. Further, it should be noted that the employment components were smaller and the real wage components larger for each of the departments of police, fire, and environmental protection than was the case for any of the departments of social services, education, or higher education.

For uniformed-delivery personnel in the six department combined, 32.3 percent of the increase in payroll costs can be attributed to changes in employment, 47.6 percent to changes in prices, and 20.1 percent to changes in real wages. In this job category the employment component ranged from 3.5 percent in fire to 74.9 percent in higher education. The price component varied from 19.4 percent in higher education to 60.8 percent in EPA. The real wage component ranged between 5.6 percent for higher education to 41.6 percent for fire.

In contrast to the uniformed-delivery category, the remaining job categories registered higher employment components for the six departments combined. The largest employment component was recorded by the executive category— 77.7 percent for all departments combined—ranging from 83.6 percent in education to 44.9 percent in fire. The clerical category also produced a large employment component—76.2 percent for the departments combined—ranging from a high of 79.7 percent in both social services and higher education to a low of 28.7 percent in fire. The smallest employment component (other than in uniformed-delivery) was registered by the laborer category—40.8 percent— ranging from 81.7 percent in social services to 2.7 percent in EPA.

For the departments combined, lower real wage components were also registered for each of the nonuniformed-nondelivery categories than was the case for the uniformed-delivery personnel. The largest real wage component in the former group was registered by the laborer category (8.4 percent) ranging from −5.1 percent in education to 33.1 percent in EPA.[g] Almost as large a real wage

[f]The index using July, 1964 as a base was 141.3 in June, 1972.

[g]The negative component is the result of a decline in the real wages for these employees. This component can be interpreted to mean that this decrease in real wages actually caused labor costs to decrease by an amount equivalent to 5.1 percent of the actual increase in labor costs over the period.

Table 4-4

The Components of Payroll Cost Change by Department and Job Category: 1965-1972

	Dollar Change in Payroll Cost	Percentage of Department Total	Percentage Due to Employment Change	Percentage Due to Price Change	Percentage Due to Real Wage Change
Police					
Executive	$ 216,206	0.1%	57.1%	39.9%	3.0%
Uniformed	229,674,525	93.8	24.2	47.1	28.7
Laborer	6,558,202	2.7	53.3	40.4	6.3
Clerical	2,829,788	1.2	73.2	30.2	-3.4
Other	5,518,868	2.3	97.3	6.3	-3.6
TOTAL	244,797,589	(17.1)	29.2	52.1	18.7
Fire					
Executive	108,774	0.1	44.9	36.6	18.5
Uniformed	103,458,875	94.8	3.5	54.9	41.6
Laborer	1,963,360	1.8	30.0	63.2	6.8
Clerical	701,154	0.6	28.7	70.0	1.3
Other	2,893,167	2.7	63.0	36.7	0.3
TOTAL	109,125,330	(7.6)	5.9	55.2	38.9
Environmental Protection					
Executive	965,005	0.8	65.2	24.9	9.9
Uniformed	69,071,567	58.9	8.6	60.8	30.6
Laborer	29,835,546	25.4	2.7	64.3	33.1
Clerical	5,352,565	4.6	50.4	41.8	7.8
Other	12,077,409	10.3	48.2	36.7	15.1
TOTAL	117,293,092	(8.2)	12.8	59.2	28.0

Table 4-4 (cont.)

	Dollar Change in Payroll Cost	Percentage of Department Total	Percentage Due to Employment Change	Percentage Due to Price Change	Percentage Due to Real Wage Change
Social Services					
Executive	841,394	0.4	61.2	29.2	9.6
Uniformed	82,375,397	40.2	46.1	33.2	20.7
Laborer	7,966,669	3.9	81.7	16.7	1.6
Clerical	71,738,679	35.0	79.7	18.5	1.8
Other	42,017,179	20.5	68.1	19.8	12.1
TOTAL	204,939,318	(14.3)	65.1	28.2	6.7
Public Schools					
Executive	5,451,802	0.1	83.6	19.4	-3.0
Delivery	487,373,827	86.1	36.9	49.0	14.1
Laborer	13,204,032	2.3	58.5	46.6	-5.1
Clerical	28,785,644	5.1	74.9	25.7	-0.6
Other	31,221,044	5.5	52.9	44.4	2.7
TOTAL	566,036,044	(39.6)	41.4	48.1	10.5

Higher Education

Executive	2,873,511	1.5	82.8	17.8	-0.6
Delivery	129,143,155	68.5	74.9	19.4	5.6
Laborer	11,111,211	5.8	64.2	28.5	7.3
Clerical	18,180,432	9.6	79.7	15.3	5.0
Other	27,165,735	14.4	76.6	13.5	9.9
TOTAL	188,474,044	(13.2)	74.8	19.4	5.8

Six Departments Combined

Executive	10,447,692	0.7	77.7	22.0	0.3
Delivery-Uniformed	1,101,076,298	77.0	32.3	47.6	20.1
Laborer	70,639,020	4.9	40.8	50.8	8.4
Clerical	127,588,262	8.9	76.2	22.2	1.6
Other	120,893,402	8.5	64.3	28.3	7.4
TOTAL	1,430,665,722	(100.0)	43.8	43.7	12.7

Source: Calculated from figures contained in Tables 4-1 and 4-2.

component occurred for the other category—7.4 percent—ranging from —3.6 percent in police to 15.1 percent in EPA. Much smaller real wage components were reported for the executive and clerical categories. In the former, the real wage component varied from —0.6 percent in higher education to 18.5 percent in fire, averaging 0.3 percent for all departments. For the latter, the range was from —3.4 percent in police to 7.8 percent in EPA, averaging 1.6 percent for the departments combined.

In general, lower price components were also obtained for each of the nonuniformed-nondelivery categories than was the case for uniformed-delivery personnel. For the exception, the laborer category, the price component averaged 50.8 percent (in contrast to 47.6 percent for uniformed-delivery personnel), and varied from 16.7 percent in social services to 64.3 percent in EPA. For each of the remaining job categories, the price component was smaller than was the case for the uniformed-delivery category. The largest price component for the remaining categories was obtained for the other category— 28.3 percent—ranging between 6.3 percent for police and 44.4 percent for education. The smallest price components were registered by the executive (22.0 percent) and clerical (22.2 percent) categories. For executive, the range was between 17.8 percent in higher education and 39.9 percent in police. For clerical employees, the price component varied between 15.3 percent for higher education and 70 percent for the fire department.

Nonpayroll Costs

Nonpayroll costs can be analyzed in an analogous fashion. Here the desire is to divide growth in nonpayroll costs into amounts due to growth in prices and that due to increased real expenditure. In other words

$$\Delta NC = n_1 \Delta P + n_2 \Delta Q' \tag{4.8}$$

where:

NC = nonpayroll costs

Q' = real expenditures

$$dNC = \lim_{\Delta \to 0} (P + \Delta P)(Q' + \Delta Q') - PQ' \tag{4.9}$$

$$= P \Delta Q' + Q \Delta P' + \Delta P \Delta Q'$$

As before, the allocation of the term involving two deltas (Δ) among the other two terms is all that is necessary to transform Equation (4.9) into (4.8). Again, for convenience, *each* of the two components (price and real expenditure) will be expressed as a percentage of the total change in nonpayroll expenditure.

These components for the six departments under study are presented in Table 4-5. As indicated there, for the six departments combined, 44.5 percent of the increase in nonpersonnel costs could be attributed to increases in prices and 54.5 percent to increased real expenditures. Increased prices were the more important cause of expenditure growth in police, fire, and education, while increased real expenditures were predominant in environmental protection, higher education, and social services. Increased prices were predominant in environmental protection, higher education, and social services. Increased prices were the least important cause of nonpayroll cost growth in higher education and the most important one in fire.

Explaining Growth in Wages, Employment, and Nonpayroll Costs

In the previous section, growth in expenditures was divided into wage, employment, and nonpayroll components in order to determine the relative importance of each in producing that growth. Ideally, the task here would be to apply the basic model presented in Chapter 2 to explain the previous growth in these three important variables (wages, employment, and nonpayroll costs). However, the time required to transform budget data to allow such a statistical estimation was so great as to lead to the rejection of this alternative. Therefore, only rough comparisons are attempted here.

Wage Growth in Public and Private Sectors

The model employed to explain expenditure growth would suggest that growth in public-employee wages would result from increases in the wages of comparable workers in the private sector. The rationale for this relationship was based upon the fact that competition for the same workers would tend to eliminate wage differentials as well as the possibility of a demonstration effect from private-sector unions wage demands to those in the public sector. In either case, wage increases in the private sector would tend to roll out into the public sector.

To investigate the nature of this relationship, average wages for the representative group of occupations in the private sector for the years 1965 and 1972 are presented in Table 4-6. The choice of occupations included in this sample was governed by the distribution of public sector jobs, subject of course, to the

Table 4-5
The Components of Nonpayroll Cost Change by Department: 1965-1972 (Amounts in Millions of Dollars)

	Dollar Change in Nonpayroll Costs	Percentage of Six Departments	Percentage Due to Price Change	Percentage Due to Real Quantity Change
Police Department	$ 74.9	16.1%	50.4%	49.6%
Fire Department	29.7	6.4	65.9	34.1
Environmental Protection	37.6	8.1	20.8	79.2
Department of Education	204.5	43.8	64.8	35.2
Board of Higher Education	80.9	17.4	6.7	93.3
Social Services Department	38.2	8.2	11.1	88.9
Six Departments Combined	$465.8	100.0%	44.5%	54.5%

Source: Calculated from data contained in Table 4-3.

Table 4-6
The Structure and Growth in Average Wages for Selected Occupations in the Private Sector in New York City: 1965 and 1972

	1965	1972	Percentage Change
Office and Clerical			
File Clerks	$3,900	$5,720	46.7%
Secretaries	5,668	8,320	46.8
Stenographers	4,784	7,020	46.7
Typists	4,108	6,136	49.4
Mean	4,615	6,799	47.4
Unskilled Maintenance			
Guards and Watchmen	4,056	6,115	50.8
Janitors and Cleaners	4,347	6,885	58.4
Laborers	5,491	8,195	49.2
Truck Drivers	6,739	10,234	51.9
Mean	5,158	7,857	52.3
Skilled Maintenance			
Carpenters	6,698	10,254	53.1
Electricians	7,030	10,171	44.7
Stationary Engineers	7,405	11,086	49.7
Mechanics	6,822	11,066	62.2
Mean	6,989	10,644	52.3
Professional			
Accountants	9,662	14,174	46.7
Auditors	9,263	13,932	50.4
Chemists	10,560	16,325	54.6
Engineers	14,510	19,487	34.3
Mean	$10,999	$15,980	45.3%

Source: Computed from *Area Wage Survey The New York Metropolitan Area*, 1965 and 1972, U.S. Labor Department, Bureau of Labor Statistics.

limited scope of the available data. As indicated in Table 4-6, wage rates grew faster for skilled and unskilled maintenance employees and most slowly for professional employees, although the range of the difference was only 7 percentage points.[h] Fastest growth for any individual job category was that for mechanics (62.2 percent) while the slowest was recorded for engineers (34.3 percent).

[h]For a detailed description of each job classification, see *Area Wage Survey, The New York Metropolitan Area*, U.S. Department of Labor, Bulletin 1725-90, (April 1972), Occupational Descriptions Appendix.

Several interesting findings are evident when these growth rates are compared with those of New York public employees as shown in Table 4-7.[i] For the categories combined, wages in each department except for education increased more rapidly than those of any category of employees in the private sector. It can readily be seen, however, that the basic reason for this result is the large wage increases in the delivery category for public employees—the average increase for delivery personnel was almost 15 percentage points higher than that for the fastest growing private-sector groups—skilled and unskilled maintenance employees. In numerous departments and other job categories, wages grew much more slowly in the public than in the private sector. More specifically, this was true in education and higher education for executives; in police, fire, social services, and education for laborers; in police, fire, and education for clerical employees; and in police and fire for other employees. In fact, for the departments combined, public-sector wages grew more slowly than private-sector wages in all categories except for delivery and other.

Employment and Workload Growth

As presented in the discussion of the model, a factor underlying growth in employment is that of employee workload. The rationale for this relationship

Table 4-7
Growth in Wage Rates by Department and Job Category: 1965-72

Department	Job Category					
	Executive	Delivery	Laborer	Clerical	Other	Average
Police	46.6%	66.8%	50.9%	33.6%	14.1%	63.4%
Fire	69.5	85.6	48.6	42.1	41.6	82.5
Environmental Protection	66.4	70.8	70.5	53.2	64.5	69.1
Social Services	63.1	79.7	47.8	48.5	79.6	60.0
Education	31.4	61.2	34.5	39.6	45.4	50.4
Higher Education	38.7	61.8	57.5	63.9	80.6	62.4
Six Departments	41.7%	66.9%	51.5%	46.5%	58.8%	59.6%

Source: Calculated from Figures contained in Table 4-2.

[i] It should be recognized that a more complete analysis should include a comparison of growth in other types of compensation in the two sectors. For example, total compensation to public employees (including pension contributions) could have risen more rapidly than that of private-sector employees, even though wage rates of public employees grew less rapidly than those of private-sector employees. However, the difficulty in obtaining comparable data between sectors on other forms of compensation made such a comparison impossible.

was based upon the idea that as the aggregate amount of work to be done increases, employment will also increase in order to maintain some stable relation between work performed and number of employees. This result obtained from the assumption of a fixed proportions production function with constant returns to scale.

While the model hypothesizes a constant relationship between output and employment, the well-known difficulty in measuring public-sector output necessitates the choice of employee workload as a proxy for output. (The obvious problem with this choice is that workload does not always correspond to output. For example, as class size increases, teacher workload also increases, but output in the form of student achievement might actually decline. However, the measurement of output—if possible—is certainly beyond the scope of this study. As a result, the shortcomings of the use of workload as a proxy for output should be recognized.) Although workload is somewhat easier to measure than output, problems still arise because of the large number of activities performed in each department. For the purposes here, the choice of workload measures for each department was based upon a determination of the activity which was most basic to that department. Hence the choice of the number of felony cases for police, number of fires for the fire department, and so forth.

The data in Table 4-8 show several measures of growth in employee workload for each department.[j] As indicated there, workload in social services increased most rapidly while that of education increased most slowly. A prime reason for the rapid growth in social service workload can be traced to the increase in aid to dependent children, which showed a 216.5 percent increase in cases over the period. A large increase in workload, the second largest of any department, was also registered by police. It should also be noted that the most serious felonies—murder, manslaughter, and homicide—increased more rapidly than any other felony category shown.

The data in Table 4-9 present growth in employment rates by department and job category. As reported earlier, growth rates in police, fire, and environmental protection, as well as in the delivery job category were slower than was the case for the other departments and job categories.

A comparison of employment and workload growth indicates that for the departments of police, fire, EPA, and social services workload increased more rapidly than employment. For education and higher education employment rose more rapidly than workload. Finally, on the average, workload increased faster than either aggregate employment or employment of uniformed-delivery personnel.

---

[j]The use of the years 1964-71 for service load was necessitated by the lack of adequate data for the later period and not a desire to argue for a one-year lag in the employment response to service load changes. Because of the rough nature of the comparisons of this chapter, such a consideration of lags was omitted.

Table 4-8

Growth in New York City Government Workload by Department: 1964-1971

	1964	1971	Percentage Change
Police			
Murder, Manslaughter and Homicide	558	1,466	163.8%
Robbery and Burglary	114,935	270,325	135.2
Grand Larceny	105,611	165,104	56.3
Other Felonies	38,210	73,153	91.4
Total Felony Cases	259,314	510,048	96.7%
Fire			
Residential Fires	23,609	33,494	41.9%
Rubbish Fires	21,219	45,669	115.2
Other Fires	34,649	46,143	33.2
Total Fires	79,477	125,306	57.7%
Environmental Protection			
Tons of Household Rubbish	2,488,577	3,146,801	26.4%
Tons of Other Rubbish	445,873	638,190	43.1
Total Tons	2,934,450	3,784,991	29.0%
Education			
Enrollment 1-8	726,767	780,811	7.4%
Enrollment 9-12	327,434	357,631	9.2
Total Enrollment	1,054,201	1,138,442	8.0%
Higher Education			
Enrollment 2-year	44,820	98,203	119.1%
Enrollment 4-year	77,037	106,953	38.8
Total Enrollment	121,857	205,156	68.4%
Social Services			
Cases of Aid to Dependent Children	76,062	240,763	216.5%
Old Age Cases	32,397	75,240	132.2
Other Cases	65,225	158,538	143.1
Total Cases	173,684	474,541	173.2%
Six Departments			
Average Workload			72.2%

Source: *Police:* City of New York Police Department, *Annual Report*, 1964 and 1971 (New York City: City of New York Police Department).

Table 4-8 (cont.)

Fire: City of New York Fire Department, *Annual Report*, 1964 and 1971 (New York City: City of New York Fire Department).

EPA: New York City Department of Sanitation, *Annual Progress Report and Statistical Review*, 1964 and 1971, (New York City: New York City Department of Sanitation).

Education: Unpublished tables of the Bureau of Education Data Systems, New York State Department of Education.

Higher Education: Unpublished tables of the Bureau of Education Data Systems, New York State Department of Education.

Social Services: Statistical Supplement to the Annual Report of 1971 (Albany, New York: New York State Department of Social Services).

Employment and Nonpayroll Cost Growth

Since the relative levels of labor and nonlabor costs for each department have been discussed previously, the focus of this subsection is to compare growth in labor and nonlabor costs. More specifically, Table 4-10 provides a comparison of the growth in employment and nonlabor costs between 1965 and 1972.[k] Although there is no proportional relationship apparent, these data do point to some conclusions consistent with the above-mentioned model. Particularly, in fire, growth in employment and nonlabor costs were both lowest of all functions. Further, growth in both employment and nonlabor costs was largest in higher education and second largest in social services.

Table 4-9
Growth in New York City Government Employment by Department and Job Category: 1965-1972

Department	Job Category					
	Executive	Delivery	Laborer	Clerical	Other	Average
Police	62.5%	19.3%	53.2%	98.6%	673.3%	23.6%
Fire	50.0	2.3	23.6	17.0	70.9	5.0
Environmental Protection	108.0	6.3	1.9	49.7	49.5	9.4
Social Services	92.3	56.7	182.6	176.5	141.0	114.6
Education	171.0	31.3	50.4	115.3	52.1	37.1
Higher Education	173.8	155.2	91.7	215.4	216.2	161.0
Six Departments	147.3%	28.4%	33.8%	146.8%	100.8%	41.3%

Source: Calculated from figures contained in Table 4-1.

[k]In terms of the theory presented in Chapter 2, this comparison should be made in terms of employment and nonlabor quantities (rather than costs). However, due to the fact that the determination of quantities is beyond the scope of this analysis, costs are used as a proxy. An interesting attempt at measuring nonlabor quantities implicitly after calculation of a price index was made in Greytak and Dinkelmeyer (27). These estimates could not be used here because they relate to different departments over a different time period.

Table 4-10
Employment and Nonpayroll Growth by Function: 1965-1972

Department	Employment Growth	Nonpayroll Cost Growth
Police	23.6%	81.6%
Fire	05.0	62.4
Environmental Protection	09.4	197.9
Local Schools	37.1	63.4
Higher Education	161.0	612.9
Social Services	114.6	370.9
Six Departments Combined	41.3	92.3

Source: Calculated from figures in Tables 4-1 and 4-3.

Forecasting Expenditure Growth

Previous sections have been concerned with an analysis of past growth in New York City expenditures. Of equal interest to academicians and policymakers alike is the forecasting of future growth. The purpose here is to demonstrate the forecasting abilities of the basic model.[1] If we begin with the equations:

$$LC = E \cdot W' \cdot P \qquad (4.10)$$

$$NC = P \cdot Q' \qquad (4.11)$$

then it was shown above that

$$\Delta LC = l_1 \Delta E + l_2 \Delta W' + l_3 \Delta P \qquad (4.12)$$

$$\Delta NC = n_1 \Delta P + n_2 \Delta Q' \qquad (4.13)$$

If we further assume (as done in Chapter 2) that

$$Q' = c_1 \Delta E \qquad (4.14)$$

then, if $n_3 = c_1 n_2$

$$\Delta NC = n_1 \Delta P + n_3 \Delta E \qquad (4.13A)$$

Since the total change in expenditures (ΔX) is merely the sum of changes in labor (ΔLC) and nonlabor costs (ΔNC), then

---

[1]For a more complete discussion of this application see Bahl and Gustely (7).

$$\Delta X = \Delta LC + \Delta NC \tag{4.15}$$

$$= l_1 \Delta E + l_2 \Delta W' + l_3 \Delta P + n_1 \Delta P + n_3 \Delta E$$

$$= (l_1 + n_3) \Delta E + l_2 \Delta W' + (l_3 + n_1) \Delta P$$

In other words, the total change in expenditure can be attributed to changes in employment, real wages and prices.

This expression (Equation 4.15) should suggest a means of obtaining estimates of expenditures into the future. The method requires estimates of future levels of employment, wages, and prices. Forecasts could equally well be obtained for individual departments or for city governments as a whole.

The attraction of this approach to expenditure forecasts should be apparent. With a minimum of data, it is possible to arrive at forecasts of future expenditure levels. And it is obviously possible, if these forecasts are considered too rough in character, to further disaggregate expenditures in a similar fashion. For example, with adequate data, it would be possible to analyze, in a similar fashion, growth in pension costs, transfer payments, and so forth.

It is at this point that the need for further research becomes evident. Specifically, without any time-series analysis of the determinants of wages and employment for particular cities, the estimation of future levels of these variables becomes nothing more than guesswork. A logical place to begin such an analysis would certainly involve an application of the model presented and tested above to time-series data. However, the unavailability of such detailed data of a sufficient time span makes this task beyond the scope of the present study. Still, it should be recognized that the present analysis has laid a foundation for such a study and provided valuable insights into the understanding of factors underlying expenditure growth for a particular city.

5

The Municipal Expenditure Determination Process in Perspective

As indicated at the beginning of this study, the understanding of the severity of the municipal fiscal crisis, as well as the formulating of likely solutions to that crisis, requires the synthesis of the wage, employment, and expenditure determinants studies into a comprehensive theory of the municipal expenditure determination process. Accordingly, the purpose of this study has been to derive a model to describe that process of expenditure determination and to test its ability to explain both cross-sectional and time-series variations in city government expenditures. The focus of this chapter is to assess the importance of these results, and, where possible, to compare them with those of other studies. Specifically, the present task is to discuss the significance of both the cross-sectional and time-series results and to describe their implications for public policy, as well as for the direction of further research in the analysis of expenditure variation.

Significance of the Cross-Section Results

In order to place the cross-sectional results in perspective and to compare them with those obtained in previous studies, forecasting equations for each of the important variables (wages, employment, and nonpayroll costs) are presented in Tables 5-1, 5-2, and 5-3. These equations are those obtained from step-wise regressions and contain only *significant* variables.

These equations suggest two very important conclusions concerning the implications drawn from previous determinants studies. First, the positive relationship between the income and expenditure variables found in many of these studies appears to result from the effect of the former variable on public-employee wages rather than upon employment levels. The only significant relationship found in the employment equation between income and employment was negative, indicating that the variable might be measuring need for the service. In any event, the conclusion derived from many studies, indicating that the positive income variable suggests an income elastic demand for public goods would seem to be erroneous if those demands are expected to result in increased employment. It is possible that wage increases could be obtained by employees in return for a better quality or quantity of services provided per employee. However, because of the difficulty in measuring the amount of services performed, let alone their quality, such a determination is beyond the scope of this study.

73

Table 5-1
Cross-Section Wage Forecasting Equations

		R^2

Police

1966 1.1855 *SERV1* + 29.9403 *UNION* + 1499.57   0.6612
(0.1712)   (12.0510)
[0.7027]   [0.2521]

1971 1.3355 *SERV2* + 54.7306 *UNION* +   780.83   0.6813
(0.1962)   (16.1394)
[0.6676]   [0.3325]

Fire

1966 1.1587 *SERV1* + 0.6489 *INC1* + 30.9352 *UNION* − 3672.83   0.7912
(0.1698)   (0.1582)   (11.7388)
[0.5792]   [0.3541]   [0.2196]

1971 1.7191 *SERV2* + 2064.8970 *WEST* + 949.6567 *CENT* −
(0.2279)   (433.8392)   (357.1010)   197.6065   0.7466
[0.6767]   [0.4507]   [0.2463]

Common Functions

1966 1.0528 *SERV1* + 0.5767 *INC1* − 963.2708 *SOUTH* − 2145.49   0.7374
(0.1879)   (0.1875)   (283.6664)
[0.5238]   [0.3133]   [0.3241]

1971 1.4389 *SERV2* − 1620.8731 *SOUTH* + 937.5386 *WEST* +
(0.1951)   (335.1445)   (365.9881)   1773.23   0.7693
[0.6278]   [0.4092]   [0.2268]

Note: Figures in parentheses are standard errors and those in brackets are beta coefficients.

Second, the positive significance of aid variables reported in other studies appears to be a result of its relationship to employment and not to wages. In no wage equation, even when the opportunity wage variable was excluded, was the aid variable significant. However, in four of the six forecasting equations, aid was significantly and positively related to employment.

In assessing the implications of these findings concerning the impact of aid, several facts should be emphasized. Most of the common functions studied here (except for highways) receive no substantial amounts of aid from outside sources. As a consequence, nothing can be concluded here about the existence (or absence) of direct expenditure stimulation resulting from outside aid. Rather, the positive significance of the aid variable might suggest that cities with greater reliance on outside assistance for aided functions are free to allocate larger amounts of money to nonaided functions than are those with a lesser reliance on outside aid.

Further, it should be noted that the aid variable employed here is defined as

Table 5-2
Cross-Section Employment Forecasting Equations

	R^2

Police

1966 0.0354 *AIDP1* + 0.0404 *FELP1* − 0.5957 *WEST* + 0.7662   0.4096
      (0.0110)   (0.0129)   (0.2984)
      [0.4195]   [0.4210]   [−0.2683]

1971 −0.0005 *INC2* − 0.0006 *WP2* − 1.0321 *WEST* + 2.7844   0.4417
      (0.0002)   (0.0001)   (0.4312)
      [−0.3658]   [0.7212]   [−0.3345]

Fire

1966 0.0171 *AIDP1* + 0.0589 *FIRP1* + 0.7480   0.4667
      (0.0059)   (0.0127)
      [0.3530]   [0.5657]

1971 −0.0002 *INC2* + 0.0637 *FIRP2* + 3.1221   0.4801
      (0.0001)   (0.0147)
      [−0.2895]   [0.5467]

Common Functions

1966 0.0649 *AIDP1* − 0.0012 *INC1* + 0.0776 + 15.2530   0.3986
      (0.0277)   (0.0004)   (0.0270)
      [0.3080]   [−0.3670]   [0.3783]

1971 0.0789 *AIDP2* + 3.0186 *SOUTH* + 0.0696 *NEED2* + 3.6080   0.3913
      (0.0301)   (0.9493)   (0.0206)
      [0.3666]   [0.4465]   [0.4486]

Note: Figures in parentheses are standard errors and those in brackets are beta coefficients.

the fraction of general revenues received in outside aid as opposed to per capita outside aid used in other studies. The use of per capita aid has been criticized by Morss (44) and others because of the possibility that it introduces circularity in the model, because of the inclusion of aid funds on both sides of the equation. As a result, the greater the amount of aid, the more difficult it is to compare the results obtained here with those of studies using the per capita specification. However, this problem of circularity is of much less consequence in the present study because of the fact that the functions under study are essentially nonaided.

In spite of the problems just discussed, it can be concluded that the results obtained here are consistent with others investigating the impact of aid on nonaided functions. For example, Bahl (2) (for police, fire, and the common functions) and Sacks and Harris (54) (for the nonaided functions) found aid to be positively related to nonaided expenditures, indicating a reallocation of expenditures toward these functions. In addition, the results of this study suggest that the primary effect of this aid is through its impact on employment rather than wage rates.

Table 5-3
Cross-Section Nonpayroll Cost Forecasting Equations

	R^2
Police	
1966 960.5086 *EPP1* + 4297.2896 *WEST* + 889.81 (461.2623) (1024.2539) [0.2853] [0.5748]	0.3489
1971 8071.7344 *EPP2* − 10594.1375 (1023.6981) [0.7918]	0.6267
Fire	
1966 2351.8026 *EFP1* − 2.0148 *COST1* + 3249.7817 *WEST* + (731.4838) (0.7650) (897.6466) 16433.0116 [0.4809] [−0.4059] [0.5226]	0.3580
1971 1.7750 *COST2* − 12818.1209 (0.8797) [0.3149]	0.0990
Common Functions	
1966 8934.1954 *WEST* + 23651.3731 (4182.4737) [0.3313]	0.1097
1971 9310.5591 *ECP2* − 51036.7867 (1639.3993) [0.6824]	0.4656

Note: Figures in parentheses are standard errors and those in brackets are beta coefficients.

Besides their important relationships to previous studies, these cross-sectional results suggest conclusions not obtainable from these other studies. The elasticity data in Table 5-4 suggest such conclusions. The fact that larger coefficients were obtained for the opportunity wage than was the case for workload might be indicative of the fact that labor market conditions exert more influence over wages than does the political process over employment. If nothing else, they suggest that public-sector wages are more responsive to external influence than is public employment.

It is also interesting to note that, while the employment elasticity coefficients of nonpayroll costs varied widely, they were larger than the other elasticities in four of the six cases. This responsiveness might be a result of the complementary nature of labor and nonlabor inputs in the production process, or the fact that with added employment comes city responsibility to provide pension and fringe benefit coverage for its employees.

The wage elasticities of public employment as indicated in Table 5-4 also suggest some interesting conclusions. While elasticities that were different from

Table 5-4
Estimates of Cross-Section Elasticity Coefficients

	Police	Fire	Common Functions
Opportunity Wage Elasticity of Public Wages			
1966	0.7269[a]	0.6081	0.4796
1971	0.6206	0.7886	0.6901
Service Needs Elasticity of Public Employment			
1966	0.3029	0.3329	0.1685[b]
1971	0.1094[b]	0.4237	0.2753
Public Employment Elasticity of Nonpayroll Costs			
1966	0.7497	1.7642	0.3893
1971	1.9277	0.4355	1.9964
Public Wage Elasticity of Public Employment			
1966	−0.5689[b]	−0.5843	−0.3460[b]
1971	−0.9250[b]	−0.5340	−0.3514[b]
Public Wage Elasticity of Public Expenditures			
1966	0.7981	1.4977	2.4959
1971	0.6620	0.3479	0.6735
Public Employment Elasticity of Public Expenditures			
1966	0.8786	1.0892	0.8345
1971	1.1566	0.8907	1.3100

[a]The elasticity coefficients are calculated at the mean.
[b]These coefficients are not significantly different from zero.

zero were obtained for fire, the insignificance of the coefficient for police and the common functions produced zero elasticities in these cases. Further, even in the case of fire, the coefficients suggest an inelastic demand for labor. It should also be noted that the wage elasticities calculated here are only slightly different from those found by Ehrenberg (18) for state and local police and fire employees. Both these studies suggest the existence of a significant disemployment effect of wage increases for some functions, however, in both cases, the size of the effect is quite small.

Finally, this study yields some important conclusions concerning the relative effect of wage or employment increases on expenditures. When the wage and employment elasticities are calculated as follows:

$$n_w = \frac{dX_p^i}{dW^i} \cdot \frac{W^i}{X_p^i} \quad \text{and} \quad n_E = \frac{dX_p^i}{dE_p^i} \cdot \frac{E_p^i}{X_p^i}$$

where:

$$\frac{dX_p^i}{dW^i} = \frac{dPC_p^i}{dW^i} + \frac{dNC_p^i}{dW^i} = E_p^i \frac{dW^i}{dW^i} + W \frac{dE_p^i}{dW^i} + \frac{dNC_p^i}{dE_p^i} \cdot \frac{dE_p^i}{dW^i}$$

$$\frac{dX_p^i}{dE_p^i} = \frac{dPC_p^i}{dE_p^i} + \frac{dNC_p^i}{dE_p^i} = E_p^i \frac{dW^i}{dE_p^i} + W \frac{dE_p^i}{dE_p^i} + \frac{dNC_p^i}{dE_p^i}$$

and where:

X_p^i = expenditures per 1000 population in function i

W^i = average public-employee wage rate in function i

E_p^i = public employment per 1000 population in function i

PC_p^i = payroll costs per 1000 population in function i

NC_p^i = nonpayroll costs per 1000 population in function i

the results as presented in Table 5-4 are obtained. Worthy of specific note is the fact that the elasticity coefficients for employment for most functions are larger and for other functions more than double those for wages. Therefore these results imply that at the margin the dominant influence on city expenditures (at least for the cities in the sample) has been exerted by employment rather than wages.

Significance of the Time-Series Results

The significance of the time-series results can be more easily seen from the forecasting equations and elasticity coefficients shown in Tables 5-5 and 5-6. The elasticity coefficients in Table 5-6 which focus upon the marginal effects of real wages, employment, and prices (derived from the equations in Table 5-5) are of particular importance. In every department, wage elasticities were greater than those for employment. However, the significance of these results is that,

Table 5-5
Time-Series Payroll and Nonpayroll Forecasting Equations

Police

$$\Delta LC = 10,794\,\Delta E + 3,103,152\,\Delta P + 33,834\,\Delta W'$$
$$\Delta NC = 917,275\,\Delta P + 5,625\,\Delta E$$
$$\Delta X = 16,419\,\Delta E + 4,020,427\,\Delta P + 33,834\,\Delta W'$$

Fire

$$\Delta LC = 9,145\,\Delta E + 1,465,625\,\Delta P + 17,021\,\Delta W'$$
$$\Delta NC = 476,886\,\Delta P + 14,431\,\Delta E$$
$$\Delta X = 23,576\,\Delta E + 1,942,511\,\Delta P + 17,021\,\Delta W'$$

Environmental Protection

$$\Delta LC = 8,463\,\Delta E + 1,689,477\,\Delta P + 22,587\,\Delta W'$$
$$\Delta NC = 189,781\,\Delta P + 16,782\,\Delta E$$
$$\Delta X = 25,245\,\Delta E + 1,879,258\,\Delta P + 22,587\,\Delta W'$$

Education

$$\Delta LC = 10,669\,\Delta E + 6,624,416\,\Delta P + 77,287\,\Delta W'$$
$$\Delta NC = 3,223,844\,\Delta P + 3,270\,\Delta E$$
$$\Delta X = 13,939\,\Delta E + 9,848,260\,\Delta P + 77,287\,\Delta W'$$

Higher Education

$$\Delta LC = 13,350\,\Delta E + 889,634\,\Delta P + 8,085\,\Delta W'$$
$$\Delta NC = 131,387\,\Delta P + 7,148\,\Delta E$$
$$\Delta X = 20,498\,\Delta E + 1,021,021\,\Delta P + 8,085\,\Delta W'$$

Social Services

$$\Delta LC = 8,014\,\Delta E + 1,406,153\,\Delta P + 17,672\,\Delta W'$$
$$\Delta NC = 102,190\,\Delta P + 2,043\,\Delta E$$
$$\Delta X = 10,057\,\Delta E + 1,508,343\,\Delta P + 17,672\,\Delta W'$$

when cost-of-living wage increases are accounted for, employment elasticities are generally greatest, while *real* wage elasticities are smallest in every case. The importance of this distinction should be recognized by critics of city governments (particularly New York City) who argue that the basic cause of expenditure increases is wage increases.

The time-series elasticity coefficients shown in Table 5-7 provide an interesting comparison with those derived from cross-sectional data (Table 5-4). While these are only rough approximations, the relationship among the three sets of

Table 5-6
Expenditure Elasticity Coefficients with Respect to Independent Variables

Department	Employment	Prices	Real Wages
Police	1.3956	1.2187	0.8763
Fire	1.9568	1.1474	0.8545
Environmental Protection	2.8022	1.3462	1.1858
Education	0.9200	1.0996	0.7342
Higher Education	1.5169	1.1524	0.8093
Social Services	1.6292	1.6872	1.1451

coefficients is quite similar to those reported earlier, that is, the elasticities of wages are generally greater than those for employment, while those for nonpayroll costs are largest of all. The most basic difference between the time-series and cross-sectional results is the fact that the wage elasticity coefficients for the former are greater than one, while those for cross-sectional data are all less than one. This would seem to indicate that, at least for New York, public-employee wages might be more responsive to private-sector wages than for other cities.

Implications for Public Policy

With the knowledge gained in the cross-sectional and time-series analysis of the expenditure determination process, it is possible to focus on the implications of these results for public policy. Specifically, it remains to be demonstrated how changes in the determinants of wages, employment levels, and public expenditures might have exacerbated the municipal fiscal crisis, and further, what these changes imply regarding public policy to alleviate this crisis.

Table 5-7
Estimates of Time-Series Elasticity Coefficients

Department	% Δ Wages / % Δ Opportunity Wage	% Δ Employment / % Δ Workload	% Δ Nonpayroll Cost / % Δ Employment
Police	1.2122	0.2440	3.4576
Fire	1.5774	0.0866	12.4800
Environmental Protection	1.3212	0.3241	21.0531
Local Schools	1.0632	4.6375	1.7088
Higher Education	1.3774	2.3538	3.8068
Social Services	1.2658	0.6616	3.2364

First, it has been shown that wage rollout from the prviate into the public sector is an important factor in the determination of these rates. Further, it has also been demonstrated both here and elsewhere that the rate of inflation can be an important determinant of wage rates, both public and private. Given the well-accepted notion that price stabilization is a function of the federal government (as opposed to localities), it might be argued that inflation in public wage rates (and expenditures) is due to the unwillingness (or inability) of the federal government to undertake this function. The clear implication of this result is that the federal government should provide aid to localities because of its failure to control the general price level. This argument is made in Greytak, Gustely, and Dinkelmeyer (28). Such a program might either be handled by per employee grants to the individual municipal governments, or directly to all workers through the federal personal income tax.

Second, it has also been suggested that employee workload (or citizen service need) has had an important impact upon public employment. Further, other studies have demonstrated that variation in service need (as defined in this study) can be related to variation in the wealth of the municipalities involved. Given the fact that distributional goals are generally believed to be a concern of the federal, not local government, the implication of this result is that the federal government should institute a program to insure that all localities have a similar capability of satisfying the basic service needs of its citizens. Such a program could be based upon a variable federal subsidy (depending upon fiscal capacity) to help pay wages of employees hired to provide for these service needs.

Finally, the importance of the programs just described is especially clear when recalling the expenditure elasticities reported in the previous sections. The high degree of responsiveness of expenditures to changes in employment and wages as reported there suggest that changes in the general price level as well as service need have apparently had a substantial effect on public expenditure as a whole. Therefore it seems that a case can be made for the argument that the federal government, given its failure to achieve stabilization and distributional goals through direct action, should take action to alleviate the effects of that failure on the municipalities.

Implications for Future Research

In conclusion, it would seem useful to point out some areas in which future research would be most helpful in clarifying the issues dealt with in this study. First of all, it would appear helpful to employ the model presented above to analyze municipal expenditure on other functions,[a] as well as to explain expenditures of other levels of government. Questions relating to the importance

[a]For an application of basic model to human service functions, see Bahl and Gustely (6).

of wage rollout, the significance of service needs, and the relative impact of wage and employment levels on public expenditures could then be answered if such research were undertaken.

Secondly, basic to this study was an assumption of a fixed proportions production function. It would appear, at this point, that much could be discovered by investigating alternative assumptions concerning the nature of the production function. While it is recognized that the outputs of city governments are not readily quantifiable, it would seem plausible to investigate in more depth the relationship between employment levels and various categories of nonlabor inputs (for example, materials, equipment, and supplies), as well as the possible substitutability between labor and capital inputs and among types of labor inputs.

Another comment concerning future research relates to the necessity for in-depth analyses of particular cities to be undertaken. This is especially necessary in light of the suggestions for research outlined above. It is questionable, for example, whether it would be possible to derive a cross-section production function for city governments (given the nature of the available aggregate data), not to mention the problem of interpreting the implications of such a function for any particular city. The most compelling argument for time-series analysis, then, is that the types of questions which need investigating lend themselves particularly well to this form of inquiry.

Finally, more investigation into both the effect of regional differences on expenditures and the cause of these regional differences needs to be conducted. In terms of the effects of these regional differences, additional research is required to determine their significance in explaining city government wage rates, employment levels, and nonpayroll costs for the common functions not analyzed here. As for the causes of regional variation, the relative merits of such explanations as variation in functional responsibility, as well as variation in the "tastes" for public goods, among others, need to be assessed.[b]

[b]One explanation for such variation, regional differences in governmental structure, is analyzed in Gustely (31).

Appendixes

Appendix A:
Key to Regression Variables[a]

WP	=	Average wage of police employees
WF	=	Average wage of fire employees
WC	=	Average wage of common-function employees
EPP	=	Employment in police per 1000 population
EFP	=	Employment in fire per 1000 population
ECP	=	Employment in common functions per 1000 population
SERV	=	Average earnings of private-sector employees (opportunity wage)
AIDP	=	Percentage of general revenues derived from external aid
UNION	=	Percentage of private-sector workers in the state unionized
CEN	=	Percentage of SMSA population residing in city
FELP	=	Felonies per 1000 population
FIRP	=	Fires per 1000 population
NEED	=	Fires and felonies per 1000 population
NLP	=	Nonpayroll costs per 1000 population in police
NLF	=	Nonpayroll costs per 1000 population in fire
NLC	=	Nonpayroll costs per 1000 population in the common functions
XPP	=	Current expenditures per 1000 population in police
XFP	=	Current expenditures per 1000 population in fire
XCP	=	Current expenditures per 1000 population in the common functions
COST	=	Cost of living for family of four on intermediate family budget
INC	=	Median family income
SOUTH	=	Regional dummy variable
WEST	=	Regional dummy variable
CENT	=	Regional dummy variable
UNEM	=	Percentage unemployed in SMSA

[a]The numeral one (1) following any of these variables indicates the year 1966, while the numeral two (2) indicates the year 1971.

Appendix B:
Data Sources

WP: *The Municipal Yearbook*, International City Managers Association (1967 and 1972).

WF: *The Municipal Yearbook*, International City Managers Association (1967 and 1972).

WC: *City Employment*, U.S. Department of Commerce (1967 and 1972).

EPP: *City Employment*, U.S. Department of Commerce (1967 and 1972).

EFP: *City Employment*, U.S. Department of Commerce (1967 and 1972).

ECP: *City Employment*, U.S. Department of Commerce (1967 and 1972).

SERV: *County Business Patterns*, U.S. Department of Commerce (1966 and 1971).

UNION: *Directory of National Unions and Employment Associations,* U.S. Bureau of Labor Statistics (1971)

CEN: *U.S. Census of Population*, U.S. Bureau of the Census (1960 and 1970).

INC. *U.S. Census of Population*, U.S. Bureau of the Census (1960 and 1970).

POPULATION: U.S. Census of Population, U.S. Bureau of the Census (1960 and 1970).

FELP: Uniform Crime Reports for the U.S., U.S. Department of Justice (1966 and 1971).

FIRP: "Fire Record of Cities." *Fire Journal* (April 1967 and 1972).

NEED: "Fire Record of Cities," and *Uniform Crime Reports.*

XPP: *City Government Finances*, U.S. Department of Commerce (1966 and 1971).

XFP: *City Government Finances*, U.S. Department of Commerce (1966 and 1971).

XCP: *City Government Finances*, U.S. Department of Commerce (1966 and 1971).

AIDP: *City Government Finances*, U.S. Department of Commerce (1966 and 1971).

NLP: City Government Finances, Municipal Yearbook, and *City Employment* (1966, 1967 and 1971, 1972).

NLF: City Government Finances, Municipal Yearbook, and *City Employment* (1966, 1967 and 1971, 1972).

NLC: *City Government Finances, Municipal Yearbook*, and *City Employment* (1966, 1967 and 1971, 1972).

COST: "Family Budget Studies," U.S. Bureau of Labor Statistics (1966 and 1971).

UNEM: *Area Trends in Employment and Unemployment* (September 1966 and 1971).

Appendix C:
Representative Occupations
Included in Each Job Category

Executive

Commissioner, Deputy Commissioner, Assistant Commissioner, Superintendent, Assistant Superintendent, President, Dean, Special Council, Director, Special Assistant

Uniformed

Police: Policeman

Fire: Fireman

Environmental Protection: Sanitationman

Social Services: Supervisor-Casework, Investigator-Casework

Public Schools: Principal, Teacher

Higher Education: Professor, Associate Professor, Assistant Professor, Instructor

Health Services: Doctor, Nurse, Public Health Consultant, Public Health Educator

Laborer

Motor Vehicle Operator, Auto Mechanic, General Laborer, Custodian, Cleaner, Electrician, Painter, Carpenter

Clerical

Stenographer, Typist, Clerk, Key Punch Operator, Telephone Operator, Secretary, Clerical Aide, Messenger

Other

Administrative Assistant, Engineer, Attorney, Clerk Grade 5, Accountant, Lab Technician, Photographer, Cook, Chaplain, Therapist, Dental Hygienist, Chemist

Appendix D:
The Methodology of the
Components of
Expenditure Change

In this appendix alternative methods of partitioning a change in a multiplicative variable into its components will be presented, and the effects of these procedures on the estimated contribution of the components to the change in the multiplicative variable will be analyzed. In the first subsection, the focus will be placed on the two-component case (for example, a wage rate and an employment effect); in the second, the three-component case (for example, a real wage rate, a price, and an unemployment effect) will be investigated. In the third subsection, the two- and three-component cases will be considered as special cases of the n component case. Finally, in the fourth subsection, a method for obtaining a weighted average component will be discussed.

Partitioning in a Two-Component Case

Suppose an attempt is made to determine the marginal effect on multiplicative variable, XY, of changes in X as well as Y. By the definition of the derivative:

$$d(XY) = \lim_{\Delta X, \Delta Y \to 0} (X + \Delta X)(Y + \Delta Y) - XY \qquad (D.1)$$

which, when expanded becomes:

$$d(XY) = \lim_{\Delta X, \Delta Y \to 0} XY + X\Delta Y + Y\Delta X + \Delta X\Delta Y - XY \qquad (D.2)$$

$$= \lim_{\Delta X, \Delta Y \to 0} X\Delta Y + Y\Delta X + \Delta X\Delta Y \qquad (D.2a)$$

When the limits are applied, this collapses into the total derivative of a product:

$$d(XY) = XdY + YdX \qquad (D.3)$$

Assuming, however, that ΔX and ΔY are discrete changes measured over a finite time period, the limit may not be applied, so that the expansion remains:

$$\Delta(XY) = X\Delta Y + Y\Delta X + \Delta X\Delta Y \qquad (D.4)$$

This appendix is excerpted from Gustely (30).

In terms which will be used in this analysis, the total change in XY can be partitioned into a Y component ($X\Delta Y$), and X component ($Y\Delta X$), and an interaction term ($\Delta X\Delta Y$). The Y component is the change in XY due to changes in Y; the X component is the change in XY due to changes in X; and the interaction term is that amount of the change in XY which can be specifically attributed not to either X or Y, but to simultaneous changes in each.

Empirically, it is common to attribute the total change, $\Delta(XY)$ to X and Y. However, the allocation of the total change to these two components is valid only under specific and unusual circumstances. This can be seen more clearly by assuming that the changes occurred between period 1 and period 2. Using appropriate subscripts to indicate these periods, Equation (D.4) can be written in the following way:[a]

$$X_2 Y_2 - X_1 Y_1 = X_1 \Delta Y + Y_1 \Delta X + \Delta X \Delta Y, \tag{D.4a}$$

where:

$$\Delta X = X_2 - X_1$$
$$\Delta Y = Y_2 - Y_1.$$

Referring to Equation (D.4a), it is clear that the change in XY can be totally attributed to X and Y, only if the interaction term $\Delta X\Delta Y$ is allocated to X or Y. If $\Delta X\Delta Y$ is allocated to the Y component, the result is:

$$\Delta XY = (X_1 \Delta Y + \Delta X \Delta Y) + Y_1 \Delta X \tag{D.4b}$$
$$= (X_1 + \Delta X)\Delta Y + Y_1 \Delta X$$
$$= X_2 \Delta Y + Y_1 \Delta X.$$

Similarly, if $\Delta X\Delta Y$ (the interaction term) is allocated to the X component, the result is:

$$\Delta XY = X_1 \Delta Y + (Y_1 \Delta X + \Delta X \Delta Y) \tag{D.4c}$$
$$= X_1 \Delta Y + (Y_1 + \Delta Y)\Delta X$$
$$= X_1 \Delta Y + Y_2 \Delta X.$$

In order to determine the effect of either allocation on the magnitude of the

[a]An alternative expansion can be obtained using second period weights as follows:

$$X_2 Y_2 - X_1 Y_1 = X_2 \Delta Y + Y_2 \Delta X - \Delta X \Delta Y.$$

The discussion which follows could be analogously applied to this expansion but will be omitted here.

components, it is necessary to know the sign and, in some cases, the magnitude of ΔX and ΔY. For example, if both ΔX and ΔY are positive, the component with second period weights (that to which the interaction term is allocated), will be at a maximum value, while the one with initial period weights will be at a minimum value. (In the sense used here, a maximum value refers to the largest value attributable to a component, subject to the constraint that the data are increasing functions of time.) If ΔX and ΔY are both negative, the reverse situation will hold. Only if ΔX and ΔY are different in sign is the effect of the allocation indeterminate and, in this case, dependent upon the relative magnitudes of ΔX and ΔY as well as their signs.

Partitioning in a Three-Component Case

The determination of changes in a three-component variable is slightly more complicated. Beginning as before, by definition, the total derivative of the variable XYZ can be shown as:

$$dXYZ = \lim_{\Delta X, \Delta Y, \Delta Z \to 0} (X + \Delta X)(Y + \Delta Y)(Z + \Delta Z) - XYZ \quad (D.5)$$

$$= \lim_{\Delta X, \Delta Y, \Delta Z \to 0} XYZ + XY\Delta Z + XZ\Delta Y + YZ\Delta X$$

$$+ X\Delta Y\Delta Z + Y\Delta X\Delta Z + Z\Delta X\Delta Y + \Delta X\Delta Y\Delta Z - XYZ$$

$$= \lim_{\Delta X, \Delta Y, \Delta Z \to 0} XY\Delta Z + XZ\Delta Y + YZ\Delta X + X\Delta Y\Delta Z$$

$$+ Y\Delta X\Delta Z + Z\Delta X\Delta Y + \Delta X\Delta Y\Delta Z.$$

After applying the limit, this becomes:

$$dXYZ = XYdZ + XZdY + YZdX,$$

which is merely the definition of the derivative of a product of three variables. However, given discrete changes in the variables X, Y, and Z, the limit does not apply. Therefore the change in XYZ must be represented as

$$\Delta XYZ = XY\Delta Z + XZ\Delta Y + YZ\Delta X + X\Delta Y\Delta Z + Y\Delta X\Delta Z \quad (D.6)$$

$$+ Z\Delta X\Delta Y + \Delta X\Delta Y\Delta Z.$$

These terms can be interpreted in the same fashion as in the two-component case. Specifically, the Z component ($XY\Delta Z$) is the change in XYZ due solely to changes in Z; the Y component $(XZ\Delta Y)$ is the change in XYZ due solely to changes in Y; and the X component $(YZ\Delta X)$ is the change in XYZ due only to changes in X. All the remaining terms can be referred to as interaction terms, reflecting changes in XYZ which can be attributed to simultaneous changes in groups of two or all three factors.

To illustrate the effect of allocation of the interaction terms among the components, it is helpful to assume that the changes were measured between period 1 and 2. Therefore it is possible to express ΔXYZ as:[b]

$$X_2 Y_2 Z_2 - X_1 Y_1 Z_1 = Y_1 X_1 \Delta Z + X_1 Z_1 \Delta Y + Y_1 Z_1 \Delta X \tag{D.7}$$
$$+ Z_1 \Delta X \Delta Y + Y_1 \Delta X \Delta Z + X_1 \Delta Y \Delta Z + \Delta X \Delta Y \Delta Z$$

where:

$$\Delta X = X_2 - X_1$$
$$\Delta Y = Y_2 - Y_1$$
$$\Delta Z = Z_2 - Z_1$$

and the allocation of the interaction terms to one of three components can be achieved in six different ways:

$$\Delta XYZ = X_1 Y_1 \Delta Z \quad + X_1 Z_2 \Delta Y \quad + Y_2 Z_2 \Delta X \tag{D.8a}$$
$$= X_1 Y_1 \Delta Z \quad + Y_1 Z_2 \Delta X \quad + X_2 Y_2 \Delta Z \tag{D.8b}$$
$$= X_1 Z_1 \Delta Y \quad + Z_1 Y_2 \Delta X \quad + X_2 Y_2 \Delta Z \tag{D.8c}$$
$$= X_1 Z_1 \Delta Y \quad + X_1 Y_2 \Delta Z \quad + Y_2 Z_2 \Delta X \tag{D.8d}$$
$$= Y_1 Z_1 \Delta X \quad + Y_1 X_2 \Delta Z \quad + X_2 Z_2 \Delta Y \tag{D.8e}$$
$$= Y_1 Z_1 \Delta X \quad + X_2 Z_1 \Delta Y \quad + X_2 Y_2 \Delta Z \tag{D.8f}$$

For example, Equation (D.8a) can be derived from Equation (D.7) by allocating the interaction terms as follows:

---

[b]Again, the use of second period weights is possible:

$$X_2 Y_2 Z_2 - X_1 Y_1 Z_1 = Y_2 X_2 \Delta Z + X_2 Z_2 \Delta Y + Y_2 Z_2 \Delta X - \Delta X \Delta Y Z_2 - \Delta X \Delta Z Y_2$$
$$- X_2 \Delta Y \Delta Z - \Delta X \Delta Y \Delta Z.$$

Although the following argument can be applied in this case, it will be omitted here.

$$\Delta XYZ = Y_1 X_1 \Delta Z + (X_1 Z_1 \Delta Y + X_1 \Delta Y \Delta Z) + (Y_1 Z_1 \Delta X \qquad \text{(D.9)}$$

$$+ Z_1 \Delta X \Delta Y + Y_1 \Delta X \Delta Z + \Delta X \Delta Y \Delta Z)$$

$$= Y_1 X_1 \Delta Z + X_1 (Z_1 + \Delta Z) \Delta Y + (Y_1 + \Delta Y)(Z_1 + \Delta Z) \Delta X$$

$$= X_1 Y_1 \Delta Z + X_1 Z_2 \Delta Y + Y_2 Z_2 \Delta X.$$

Equations (D.8b) through (D.8f) can be derived similarly.

As was true for the two-component cases, under certain conditions it is possible, a priori, to determine the maximum and minimum values for each component. Specifically, if ΔX, ΔY, and ΔZ are positive, second-period weights will yield maximum, and first-period weights minimum, values for each component. If ΔX, ΔY, and ΔZ are all negative, the reverse is the case. If the signs of the changes are not all the same, information concerning the magnitude of each change is necessary to determine maximum and minimum values for the components.

Partitioning in an N *Component Case*

As will be pointed out in this subsection, the two- and three-component cases are special cases of the general model which follows. Specifically, by definition the derivative of the multicative variable $\prod_i^n A^i$ (where the A^is are the components of the variable and $\prod_{i=1}^n$ represents the product of n of these components) can be described as follows:

$$d\left(\prod_{i=1}^n A^i\right) = \lim_{\Delta A^i \to 0} \prod_{i=1}^n (A^i + \Delta A^i) - \prod_{i=1}^n A^i \qquad \text{(D.10)}$$

Exactly as before, when this expression is expanded, simplified and the limit applied, we obtain:

$$d\left(\prod_{i=1}^n A^i\right) = \sum_{i=1}^n \left(\prod_{j \neq i}^n A^j\right) dA^i, \qquad \text{(D.11)}$$

which is merely the definition of the derivative of the product of n variables.

96

However, when changes are discrete over time, the limit does not apply. Therefore the general expansion for the n factor model must be represented as follows:[c]

$$
\Delta(\prod_{i=1}^{n} A^i) = \sum_{i=1}^{n} [(\prod_{j \neq i}^{n} A_1^j)\Delta A^i] + \sum_{i=1}^{n} \sum_{j>i}^{n} [(\prod_{k \neq i,j}^{n} A_1^k) \qquad (D.12)
$$

$$
(\Delta A^i)(\Delta A^j)]
$$

$$
+ \sum_{i=1}^{n} \sum_{j>i}^{n} \sum_{k>i,j}^{n} [(\prod_{m \neq i,j,k}^{n} A_1^m (\Delta A^i)(\Delta A^j)
$$

$$
(\Delta A^k)] \dots + [\prod_{i=1}^{n} \Delta A^i].
$$

This general formula for the expansion of changes in the n component variable is composed of n groups of terms (2^{n-1} terms in all) of which only four are shown. The first group represents the change in the aggregate variable

$$
(\prod_{i=1}^{n} A^i)
$$

that can be attributed solely to changes in each of the components individually—that is, ΔA^i—weighted by initial values of each of the other variables. The remaining $n-1$ groups may be considered interaction terms. The second group represents the change in the aggregate variable that can be attributed to the interaction of changes in combinations of the n components taken two at a time—that is, $(\Delta A^i) (\Delta A^j)$—weighted by initial values for each of the other variables. The third group represents changes in combinations of the n components taken three at a time—that is, $(\Delta A^i) (\Delta A^j) (\Delta A^k)$—weighted by initial values of the other variables. Each of the n groups can be explained in an analogous fashion.

As explained in the two- and three-component cases, it is possible to allocate all the interaction effects among the n components of the multiplicative variable although the process is much more complicated and is of the form:

[c]Again, this expansion can be represented by use of second period weights for each of the terms with all the interaction terms preceded by a *minus* (−). The remainder of the discussion applies equally well in either case.

$$\Delta(\prod_{i=1}^{n} A^i) = (\prod_{i=1}^{n-1} A_1^i)\Delta A^n + (\prod_{i=1}^{n-2} A_2^i)(A_2^n)\Delta A^{n-1} \qquad \text{(D.13)}$$

$$+ (\prod_{i=1}^{n-3} A_1^i)(A_2^n)(A_2^{n-1})\Delta A^{n-2} \dots$$

$$+ (\prod_{i=2}^{n} A_2^i)\Delta A^{n-(n-1)}.$$

As explained above, the second-period weights in the above expression indicate the allocation of interaction term(s) to that component.

Assuming that the ΔA^i's are all positive, it is possible to determine, a priori, that the use of second weights will maximize the particular component in question, while the use of first-period weights will have the opposite effect. If the ΔA^i's are negative, the situation is reversed. If the signs of the changes are not all the same, the maximum and minimum values of the components can only be determined if the relative magnitudes of the changes are known.

The Division of Interactions among Components

With regard to the magnitude of the interaction terms, the larger the absolute size of the change in any or all of the variables, the larger are the interaction terms relative to the total change. Conversely, the smaller the changes in the variables, the smaller are the interactions. In fact, it was shown above that, as the observed changes approach zero, the components approach the value of the corresponding derivative of the multiplicative variable, that is, the interaction term approaches zero. In addition, under some conditions, the size of the interaction term will be larger than the changes in any of the interacting variables taken separately. Specifically, if $|\Delta A^i| > 1$, the size of the interaction terms in toto will be greater than any of the individual changes (ΔA^i). Alternatively, if $|\Delta A^i| < 1$, the size of the entire interaction term will be smaller than that of any of the individual changes. Since the general n component model includes 2^{n-1} terms, of which all but n are interaction terms, this problem could be acute in large component variables.

Up to this point, the interaction terms have been considered only with respect to their existence, size, and the effects of allocating them in toto to various components. In some cases, such a procedure may be appropriate. However, where the interaction terms are allocated to one or some of the components of the multiplicative variable, care should be taken to state explicitly the criteria underlying the allocation of specific interaction terms to each component. Alternatively, it is possible to partition and allocate the interaction terms themselves among the components. Such a procedure would be appropriate when an exhaustive allocation of the change in the multiplicative variable among its components is sought and when there is no compelling rationale for the allocation of any or all of the interaction terms to specific components. While the allocation of the interaction terms to the components could be subjected to a number of criteria, the following four appear to be generally appropriate.

1. The interaction terms should be allocated to the components so as to exhaust exactly the total change in the multiplicative variable in question.
2. The interaction terms should be allocated on the basis of the relative changes which actually occurred in the components.
3. The allocation of the interaction terms should not be affected by the choice of units in which the change in the component is expressed.
4. The calculations necessary to divide the terms should be relatively simple.

The first criterion is derived from the desire to attribute the *total* change in the multiplicative variable to its components. The second arises from the desire to obtain a measure of each component on the basis of its contribution to the change in the multiplicative variable. The third criterion eliminates the possibility that the size of the component can be affected by arbitrary choice of units of measurement. The fourth is designed so as to preclude the introduction of added complexity.

A number of allocational formulas meet some of these criteria. A simple average of maximum and minimum values of the respective components might be suggested. This will meet criteria (3) and (4) but will meet (1) only when there is one interaction term in a two-component variable. Further, even in the two-component case, it will violate (2), unless the changes in the components are of equal size. Alternatively, the interaction might be equally allocated to the interacting components. This procedure would meet criteria (1), (3), and (4) but, again, would violate (2). As a third possibility, allocation might take place on the basis of the absolute changes in the components included in each interaction term. However, such an allocation, while satisfying (1), (2), and (4), would violate (3). Finally, intricate weighting procedures which satisfy (1), (2), and (3) would certainly violate (4).

An alternative formula is to allocate interaction on the basis of the relative percentage change occurring in each of the interacting components.[d] In the case

[d]This technique was used in *Local Government Finance in New York State, 1959-1969.* A report to the Temporary Commission on the Powers of Local Government (Syracuse, N.Y.: Metropolitan Studies Program, Syracuse University, December 1971), Chapter 8, Appendix A.

of the two-component variable, XY, this procedure would allocate the interaction term, $\Delta X \Delta Y$, such that the fraction

$$\frac{\dfrac{\Delta X}{X}}{\dfrac{\Delta X}{X} + \dfrac{\Delta Y}{Y}}$$

of that term would be allocated to the X component and the fraction

$$\frac{\dfrac{\Delta Y}{Y}}{\dfrac{\Delta X}{X} + \dfrac{\Delta Y}{Y}}$$

to the component. In the three-component variable, XYZ, the interaction would be allocated in a similar fashion. For example, of the interaction term, $Y_1 \Delta X \Delta Z$, the fraction

$$\frac{\dfrac{\Delta X}{X}}{\dfrac{\Delta X}{X} + \dfrac{\Delta Z}{Z}}$$

would be allocated to the X component, and the fraction

$$\frac{\dfrac{\Delta Z}{Z}}{\dfrac{\Delta X}{X} + \dfrac{\Delta Z}{Z}}$$

to the Z component. Finally for the n component variable, the procedure would be much the same. The formula would involve allocation according to the relative percentage changes in each of the interacting components. Such a formula for the general model would allocate the interactions on the basis of weights of the following form:

$$\frac{\Delta A^i}{A^i} \Bigg/ \sum_{i=1}^{n} \left(\frac{\Delta A^i}{A^i} \right)$$

Regardless of the number of components involved, this weighting formula meets each of the stated criteria. In the empirical section which follows, this procedure will be used to allocate each of the interaction terms among the interacting components of that term.

Application of the Technique

The purpose of this section is to use the components technique just described to measure those factors underlying changes in labor costs. To this end, it is helpful to consider the following multiplicative variable:

$$C_t = E_t \cdot P_t \cdot W_t' \tag{D.14}$$

where:

C_t = direct labor costs in period t

E_t = employment in period t

W_t' = real wages in period t

P_t = an index of prices in period t.

In other words, direct labor costs in any period t equal the product of the employment level, an index of prices in that period, and real wages.[e] Further, changes in labor costs (ΔC) can be attributed to changes in these variables ($\Delta E, \Delta W', \Delta P$) in the following form:

$$\Delta C = c_1 \Delta E + c_2 \Delta P + c_3 \Delta W'. \tag{D.15}$$

In this equation, $c_1 \Delta E$, $c_2 \Delta P$, and $c_3 \Delta W'$ are the employment, price, and real wage components of the change in labor cost, and c_1, c_2, and c_3 are coefficients which relate changes in the components to the total change in labor costs. The size of these coefficients depend on the allocation of the interaction terms.

Since employment, prices, and real wages (E, P, W') are all increasing functions of time, the use of second-period weights will maximize the size of the components, while first-period weights will minimize that particular component. Following this procedure, the minimum and maximum values of the components can be calculated as follows:

	Minimum	Maximum
Employment (E)	$W_1'P_1 (E_2 - E_1)$	$W_2'P_2 (E_2 - E_1)$
Component	$c_1 \Delta E$	$c_1 \Delta E$

---

[e]See Gustely (30).

Prices (P)	$E_1 W_1' (P_2 - P_1)$	$E_2 W_2' (P_2 - P_1)$
Component	$c_2 \Delta P$	$c_2 \Delta P$
Real Wages (W')	$E_1 P_1 (W_2' - W_1')$	$E_2 P_2 (W_2' - W_1')$
Component	$c_3 \Delta W'$	$c_3 \Delta W'$

When the employment component is minimized, $W_1' P_1 (E_2 - E_1)$, the interaction terms are allocated to the other components. When the employment component is maximized, $W_2' P_2 (E_2 - E_1)$, the interaction terms which involve employment changes are allocated completely to the employment component. These terms are as follows:

$$(E_2 - E_1) \qquad (W_2' - W_1') P_1 \tag{a}$$

$$(E_2 - E_1) \qquad (P_2 - P_1) W_1' \tag{b}$$

$$(W_2' - W_1') \qquad (P_2 - P_1) E_1 \tag{c}$$

$$(E_2 - E_1) \qquad (W_2' - W_1') \qquad (P_2 - P_1) \tag{d}$$

As indicated in the previous section, it is possible to allocate each of these interaction terms among the changes indicated (that is, between ΔE and $\Delta W'$, ΔE and ΔP, $\Delta W'$ and ΔP, or ΔE, $\Delta W'$, and ΔP respectively).

The division of the interaction terms for the purposes of this section was made on the basis of the relative percentage change which actually occurred in the variables in question. Specifically, the fraction

$$\frac{\dfrac{\Delta E}{E_1}}{\dfrac{\Delta E}{E_1} + \dfrac{\Delta W'}{W_1'}}$$

of (a), the fraction

$$\frac{\dfrac{\Delta E}{E}}{\dfrac{\Delta E}{E_1} + \dfrac{\Delta P}{P_1}}$$

of (b), and the fraction

$$\frac{\dfrac{\Delta E}{E_1}}{\dfrac{\Delta E}{E_1} + \dfrac{\Delta P}{P_1} + \dfrac{\Delta W'}{W_1'}}$$

of (d) were all added to the minimum employment component, $W_1' P_1 (E_2 - E_1)$.[f] Similar steps were taken to determine a weighted average for the real wage and price components.

---

[f]It is also possible to subtract 1 minus these amounts from $W_2' P_2 (E_2 - E_1)$ and obtain the same results.

Bibliography

Bibliography

1. Ashenfelter, O. "The Effect of Unionization on Wages in the Public Sector: The Case of Firemen." *Industrial and Labor Relations Review* 24 (January 1971): 191-203.
2. Bahl, Roy. *Metropolitan City Expenditures.* Lexington: University of Kentucky Press, 1968.
3. _____. "Studies on the Determinants of Public Expenditures: A Review," *Functional Federalism.* Edited by S. Mushkin and J. Cotton. Washington, D.C.: George Washington University, 1968, pp. 184-207.
4. Bahl, Roy; Campbell, Alan; and Greytak, David. *Taxes, Expenditures and the Economic Base: A Case Study of New York City.* New York: Praeger, 1974.
5. Bahl, Roy; Campbell, Alan; Greytak, David; and Wasylenko, Michael. "Intergovernmental and Functional Aspects of Public Employment Trends in the U.S." *Public Administration Review* (November/December 1972): 815-32.
6. Bahl, Roy, and Gustely, Richard. "Wage Rates, Employment Levels and State and Local Government Education and Health and Hospital Expenditures: An Analysis of Interstate Variations." In *Services to People: State Aids for the Human Services in a Federal System.* Selma Mushkin, ed. Washington, D.C.: Public Services Laboratory, Georgetown University, 1974.
7. _____. "Forecasting Urban Government Expenditures." *Proceedings of the 67th Annual Conference on Taxation of the National Tax Association,* 1974.
8. Bahl, Roy, and Saunders, Robert. "Determinants of Changes in State and Local Government Expenditures." *National Tax Journal* 18 (March 1965): 50-57.
9. Barlow, Robin. "Multivariate Studies of the Determinants of State and Local Government Expenditures in the U.S." Paper prepared for the Ford Foundation Workshop on State and Local Government Finance. Ann Arbor: University of Michigan, June 1966.
10. Barr, James, and Davis, Otto. "An Elementary Political and Economic Theory of the Expenditures of Local Governments." *Southern Economic Journal* 33 (October 1966): 149-63.
11. Beck, Morris. "Towards a Theory of Public Output in Metropolitan Areas." *Economic Record* (June 1971): 245-54.
12. Bergstrom, Theodore, and Goodman, Robert. "Private Demands for Public Goods." *American Economic Review* (June 1973): 280-296.
13. Bird, Richard. "The Determinants of State and Local Expenditures: A Review of U.S. Studies." Working Paper 6907. Toronto: Institute for Quantitative Analysis of Social and Economic Policy, University of Toronto, 1969.

105

14. Bollen, J. et al. *Exploring the Metropolitan Community.* Berkeley: University of California Press, 1961.
15. Booms, Bernard, and Hu, Teh-Wei. "Toward a Positive Theory of State and Local Public Expenditure: An Empirical Example." *Public Finance* (1971): 419-36.
16. Borcherding, Thomas, and Deacon, G. "The Demand for the Services of Non-Federal Governments." *American Economic Review* (December 1972): 891-901.
17. Brazer, Harvey. *City Expenditures in the United States.* National Bureau of Economic Research, 1959.
18. Campbell, Alan, and Sacks, Seymour. *Metropolitan America.* New York: Free Press, 1967.
19. Ehrenberg, Ronald. *The Demand for State and Local Government Employees.* Lexington, Mass.: D.C. Heath, 1972.
20. _____ . "The Demand for State and Local Government Employees." *American Economic Review* (June 1973): 366-379.
21. Fabricant, Solomon. *The Trend of Governmental Activity in the U.S. since 1900.* Washington, D.C.: National Bureau of Economic Research, 1952. Ch. 6.
22. Freund, J.L. "Wage Pressures on City Hall: The Philadelphia Experience." *Business Review* (Federal Reserve Bank of Philadelphia, March 1972): 3-17.
23. Fisher, Glenn. "Interstate Variation in State and Local Government Expenditures." *National Tax Journal* 17 (March 1964): 55-74.
24. Gramlich, Edward. "Alternative Federal Policies for Stimulating State and Local Expenditures: A Comparison of Their Effects." *National Tax Journal* 21 (June 1968): 119-29.
25. _____ . "State and Local Governments and Their Budget Constraint." *International Economic Review*, 10, no. 2 (June 1969): 163-82.
26. _____ . "The Effect of Grants on State-Local Expenditures: A Review of the Econometric Literature." *Proceedings of the 62nd Annual Conference of the National Tax Association.* Columbus, Ohio, 1970.
27. Greytak, D., and Dinkelmeyer, R. "Nonlabor Expenditures in New York City Government." Syracuse: Metropolitan Research Center, Syracuse University, 1972.
28. Greytak, David; Gustely, Richard; and Dinkelmeyer, Robert. "Inflation and City Government Expenditures." *National Tax Journal* (December 1974).
29. Gustely, Richard. "Interurban Variations in the Structure and Growth of City Government Payrolls." *Papers and Proceedings of the Northeast Regional Science Association*, Syracuse, 1973.
30. _____ . "The Components of Expenditure Change: An Analysis of the Technique and Application to City Government Labor Costs." Working Paper 16 Metropolitan Research Center, Syracuse University, 1973.
31. _____ . "The Equity and Efficiency Effects of Metropolitan Government: A Case Study of Dade County, Florida," unpublished mimeo, 1974.

32. Hawley, Amos. "Metropolitan Population and Municipal Government Expenditures in Central Cities." Reprinted in *Cities and Society*. Edited by Kott and Reiss. Glencoe, Ill.: Free Press, 1957, pp. 773-82.

33. Henderson, James. "Local Government Expenditures: A Social Welfare Analysis." *Review of Economics and Statistics* (1968): 156-63.

34. Horowitz, Anne. "A Simultaneous Equation Approach to the Problem of Explaining Interstate Differences in State and Local Government Expenditures," *Southern Economic Journal* (April 1968): 459-76.

35. Johnson, S., and Junk, P. "Sources of Tax Revenues and Expenditures in Large U.S. Cities." *Quarterly Review of Economics and Business* 10, no. 4, (Winter 1974), 7-15.

36. Kasper, Hirschel. "The Effects of Collective Bargaining on Public School Teachers' Salaries." *Industrial and Labor Relations Review* 24 (October 1970).

37. Kee, Woo Sik. "Central City Expenditures and Metropolitan Area." *National Tax Journal* 18 (December 1965): 337-53.

38. Kurnow, Ernest. "Determinants of State and Local Expenditures Reexamined." *National Tax Journal* 16 (September 1963): 252-55.

39. Landon, A., and Baird, P. "Monopsony in the Market for Public School Teachers," *American Economic Review* 61 (December 1971): 966-71.

40. Lewis, H. *Unionism and Relative Wages in the United States*. Chicago: University of Chicago Press, 1963.

41. McMahon, Walter. "An Economic Analysis of the Major Determinants of Expenditures on Public Education," *Review of Economics and Statistics* 52 (August 1970): 242-52.

42. Manvel, Allen. "Regional Differences in the Scale of State and Local Governments." *National Tax Journal* (1954): 110-120.

43. Miner, Jerry. *Social and Economic Factors in Spending for Public Education*. Syracuse: Syracuse University Press, 1963.

44. Morss, Elliot. "Some Thoughts on the Determinants of State and Local Expenditures." *National Tax Journal* 19 (March 1966): 95-104.

45. Osman, Jack. "On the Use of Intergovernmental Aid as an Expenditure Determinant." *National Tax Journal* 21 no. 4 (December 1968): 437-47.

46. Owen, J.D. "Toward a Public Employment Wage Theory: Some Econometric Evidence on Teacher Quality," *Industrial and Labor Relations Review* (January 1972): 213-22.

47. Pauly, M.V. "Public Goods and Local Governments: A General Theoretical Analysis." *Journal of Political Economy* (May/June 1970): 572-85.

48. Pidot, George. "A Principal Components Analysis of the Determinants of Local Government Fiscal Patterns." *Review of Economics and Statistics* 51 (May 1969): 176-88.

49. Pogue, T., and Sgontz, L. "The Effect of Grants in Aid on State and Local Spending." *National Tax Journal* 21 (June 1968): 90-99.

50. Popp, Dean, and Sebold, Fred. "Quasi-Returns to Scale in the Provision of Police Services." *Public Finance* 26, no. 1 (1972): 46-61.

51. Ratchford, B.U. "Recent Changes in Public Pay Policies." *National Tax Journal* (December 1972): 531-40.
52. Rhemus, Charles, and Wilner, Evan. "The Economic Results of Teacher Bargaining: Michigan's First Two Years." University of Michigan Institute of Labor and Industrial Relations, 1968.
53. Sacks, Seymour. *City Schools/Suburban Schools.* Syracuse: Syracuse University Press, 1972.
54. Sacks, Seymour, and Harris, Robert. "The Determinants of State and Local Government Expenditures and Intergovernmental Flows of Funds." *National Tax Journal* 17 (March 1964): 75-85.
55. Sacks, Seymour, and Hellmuth, William. *Financing Government in a Metropolitan Area.* Glencoe: Free Press, 1961.
56. Schmenner, Roger. "On the Determinants of Municipal Employee Wages." *Review of Economics and Statistics* (February 1973): 83-90.
57. Scott, Stanley, and Feder, Edward. "Factors Associated with Variation in Municipal Expenditure Levels." Bureau of Public Administration, University of California, 1957.
58. Seigel, Barry. "On the Positive Theory of State and Local Expenditures." *Public Finance and Welfare: Essays in Honor of C. Ward Macy.* Edited by P. Kleinsorge. Eugene: Oregon University, 1966.
59. Smith, David. "The Response of State and Local Government to Federal Grants." *National Tax Journal* 21 (September 1968): 349-57.
60. Suits, Daniel. "Interpreting Regressions Containing Dummy Variables." Technical paper presented at a Research Seminar in Quantitative Economics, University of Michigan, Ann Arbor, May 1962.
61. Sunley, E.M. "Determinants of Government Expenditures within Metropolitan Areas." *American Journal of Economics and Sociology.* (October 1971): 345-61.
62. Thompson, Wilbur. *A Preface to Urban Economics.* Baltimore: Johns Hopkins Press, 1965.
63. Thornton, R. "The Effects of Collective Negotiation on Teachers' Salaries." *Quarterly Review of Economics and Business* 11, no. 4 (Winter 1971): 37-46.
64. Weicher, John. "Aid, Expenditures and Local Government Structure." *National Tax Journal* (December 1972): 573-83.
65. Wellington, H., and Winter, R. "The Limits of Collective Bargaining in Public Employment." *Yale Law Journal* 5, no. 46 (June 1969): 1107-1127.
66. _____. "Determinants of Central City Expenditures: Some Overlooked Factors and Problems." *National Tax Journal* (December 1970): 379-96.
67. Wilde, James. "The Expenditure Effects of Grant-in-Aid Programs." *National Tax Journal* (September 1968): 34-48.
68. Wilensky, Gail. "Determinants of Local Government Spending." *Financing the Metropolis.* Edited by J. Crecine. Beverly Hills, Calif. Sage Publications, 1970, pp. 197-218.

69. Wilson, Thomas, and Eckstein, Otto. "The Determination of Money Wages in American Industry," *Quarterly Journal of Economics* (August 1962): 379-415.
70. Wood, Robert. *1400 Governments.* Boston: Harvard University Press, 1961.

Index

About the Author

Richard D. Gustely is Assistant Professor of Environmental and Urban Systems at Virginia Polytechnic Institute and State University. He received the bachelor's degree in mathematics and economics from Ohio Wesleyan University in 1967, and master's and doctoral degrees in economics from Syracuse University in 1969 and 1973 respectively. A consultant to the University of Miami on the fiscal implications of metropolitan government, he has taught at Rhode Island College and has served on the research staff of the Maxwell Research Project on the Public Finances of New York City. In addition to public employment, Professor Gustely's interests include the fiscal implications of changing urban governmental structure, and the effect of public service pricing and taxation policies on the pattern of urban development.